THE WAY OF ISRAEL
Biblical Faith and Ethics

RELIGIOUS PERSPECTIVES

Planned and Edited by

RUTH NANDA ANSHEN

RELIGIOUS PERSPECTIVES · VOLUME FIVE

THE WAY OF ISRAEL

Biblical Faith and Ethics

by James Muilenburg

Harper & Brothers Publishers · New York

Grateful acknowledgment is made to the following publishers for permission to reprint the material indicated:

Thomas Nelson & Sons, for all quotations of scripture from the *Revised Standard Version of the Bible*, copyright 1946 and 1952 by the Division of Christian Education of the National Council of Churches.

Vanguard Press, Inc., for the quotation from "Invocation" by Edith Sitwell, in *The Collected Poems of Edith Sitwell*, copyright 1946 and 1954 by Edith Sitwell.

Library of Congress catalog card number: 61-12830

CONTENTS

Religious Perspectives

VOLUMES ALREADY PUBLISHED

RELIGIOUS PERSPECTIVES
Its Meaning and Purpose

RELIGIOUS PERSPECTIVES represents a quest for the rediscovery of man. It constitutes an effort to define man's search for the essence of being in order that he may have a knowledge of goals. It is an endeavor to show that there is no possibility of achieving an understanding of man's total nature on the basis of phenomena known by the analytical method alone. It hopes to point to the false antinomy between revelation and reason, faith and knowledge, grace and nature, courage and anxiety. Mathematics, physics, philosophy, biology and religion, in spite of their almost complete independence, have begun to sense their interrelatedness and to become aware of that mode of cognition which teaches that "the light is not without but within me, and I myself am the light."

Modern man is threatened by a world created by himself. He is faced with the conversion of mind to naturalism, a dogmatic secularism and an opposition to a belief in the transcendent. He begins to see, however, that the unverse is given not as one existing and one perceived but as the unity of subject and object; that the barrier between them cannot be said to have been dissolved as the result of recent experience in the physical sciences, since this barrier has never existed. Confronted with the question of meaning, he is summoned to rediscover and scrutinize the immutable and the permanent which constitute the dynamic, unifying aspect of life as well as the principle of differentiation; to reconcile identity and diversity, immutability and unrest. He begins to recognize that just as every person descends by his particular path, so he is able to ascend, and this ascent aims at a return to the source of creation, an inward home from which he has become estranged.

It is the hope of RELIGIOUS PERSPECTIVES that the rediscovery of man will point the way to the rediscovery of God. To this end a rediscovery of first principles should constitute part of the quest. These principles, not to be superseded by new discoveries, are not those of historical worlds that come to be and perish. They are to be sought in the heart and spirit of man, and no interpretation of a merely historical or scientific universe can guide the search. RELIGIOUS PERSPECTIVES attempts not only to ask dispassionately what the nature of God is, but also to restore to human life at least the hypothesis of God and the symbols that relate to him. It endeavors to show that man is faced with the metaphysical question of the truth of religion while he encounters the empirical question of its effects on the life of humanity and its meaning for society. Religion is here distinguished from theology and its doctrinal forms and is intended to denote the feelings, aspirations and acts of men, as they relate to total reality.

RELIGIOUS PERSPECTIVES is nourished by the spiritual and intellectual energy of world thought, by those religious and ethical leaders who are not merely spectators but scholars deeply involved in the critical problems common to all religions. These thinkers recognize that human morality and human ideals thrive only when set in a context of a transcendent attitude toward religion and that by pointing to the ground of identity and the common nature of being in the religious experience of man, the essential nature of religion may be defined. Thus, they are committed to re-evaluate the meaning of everlastingness, an experience which has been lost and which is the content of that *visio Dei* constituting the structure of all religions. It is the many absorbed everlastingly into the ultimate unity, a unity subsuming what Whitehead calls the fluency of God and the everlastingness of passing experience.

These volumes seek to show that the unity of which we speak consists in a certitude emanating from the nature of man who seeks God and the nature of God who seeks man. Such certitude bathes in an intuitive act of cognition, participating in the divine essence and is related to the natural spirituality of intelligence. This is not by any means to say that there is an equivalence of all faiths in the traditional religions of human history. It is, however, to emphasize the distinction between the spiritual and the temporal which all religions acknowledge. For duration of thought is composed of instants superior to time, and is an intuition of the permanence of existence and its metahistorical reality. In fact, the symbol[1] itself found on cover and jacket of each volume of RELIGIOUS PERSPECTIVES is the visible sign or representation of the essence, immediacy and timelessness of religious experience; the one immutable center, which may be analogically related to Being in pure act, moving with centrifugal and ecumenical necessity outward into the manifold modes, yet simultaneously, with dynamic centripetal power and with full intentional energy, returning to the source. Through the very diversity of its authors, the Series shows that the basic and poignant concern of every faith is to point to, and overcome, the crisis in our apocalyptic epoch—the crisis of man's separation from man and of man's separation from God—the failure of love. The authors endeavor, moreover, to illustrate the truth that the human heart is

[1] From the original design by Leo Katz.

able, and even yearns, to go to the very lengths of God; that the darkness and cold, the frozen spiritual misery of recent time, are breaking, cracking and beginning to move, yielding to efforts to overcome spiritual muteness and moral paralysis. In this way, it is hoped, the immediacy of pain and sorrow, the primacy of tragedy and suffering in human life, may be transmuted into a spiritual and moral triumph.

RELIGIOUS PERSPECTIVES is therefore an effort to explore the *meaning* of God, an exploration which constitutes an aspect of man's intrinsic nature, part of his ontological substance. The Series grows out of an abiding concern that in spite of the release of man's creative energy which science has in part accomplished, this very science has overturned the essential order of nature. Shrewd as man's calculations have become concerning his means, his choice of ends which was formerly correlated with belief in God, with absolute criteria of conduct, has become witless. God is not to be treated as an exception to metaphysical principles, invoked to prevent their collapse. He is rather their chief exemplification, the source of all potentiality. The personal reality of freedom and providence, of will and conscience, may demonstrate that "he who knows" commands a depth of consciousness inaccessible to the profane man, and is capable of that transfiguration which prevents the twisting of all good to ignominy. This religious content of experience is not within the province of science to bestow; it corrects the error of treating the scientific account as if it were itself metaphysical or religious; it challenges the tendency to make a religion of science—or a science of religion—a dogmatic act which destroys the moral dynamic of man. Indeed, many men of science are confronted with unexpected implications of their own thought and are beginning to accept, for instance, the trans-spatial and trans-temporal nature of events and of matter itself.

RELIGIOUS PERSPECTIVES attempts to show the fallacy of the apparent irrelevance of God in history. The Series submits that no convincing image of man can arise, in spite of the many ways in which human thought has tried to reach it, without a philosophy of human nature and human freedom which does not exclude God. This image of *Homo cum Deo* implies the highest conceivable freedom, the freedom to step into the very fabric of the universe, a new formula for man's collaboration with the creative process and the only one which is able to protect man from the terror of existence. This image implies further that the mind and conscience are capable of making genuine discriminations and thereby may reconcile the serious tensions between the secular and religious, the profane and sacred. The idea of the sacred lies in what it *is*, timeless existence. By emphasizing timeless existence against reason as a reality, we are liberated, in our communion with the eternal, from the otherwise unbreakable rule of "before and after." Then we are able to admit that all forms, all symbols in religions, by their negation of error and their affirmation of the actuality of truth, make it possible to experience that *knowing* which is above knowledge, and that dynamic passage of the universe to unending unity.

The volumes in this Series seek to challenge the crisis which separates, the crisis born out of a rationalism that has left no spiritual heirs, to make reasonable a religion that binds and to present the numinous reality within the experience of man. Insofar as the Series succeeds in this quest, it will direct mankind toward a reality that is eternal and away from a preoccupation with that which is illusory and ephemeral.

For man is now confronted with his burden and his greatness: "He calleth to me, Watchman, what of the night? Watchman, what of the night?"[2] Perhaps the anguish in the human soul may be assuaged by the answer, by the *assimilation* of the person in God: "The morning cometh, and also the night: if ye will inquire, inquire ye: return, come."[3]

RUTH NANDA ANSHEN

---

[2] Isaiah 21:11.
[3] Isaiah 21:12.

THE WAY OF ISRAEL

Biblical Faith and Ethics

1
The Way of the Word

MORE THAN ANY OTHERS OF OUR AGE, IT IS THE
poets, dramatists, and tellers of stories who penetrate most
deeply into the mind and heart of contemporary man. They
have declined the office of spectator, but have chosen instead
to bring us to the place where words are spoken and heard, and
thus to engage us in that interior conversation where the walls
of our isolation and self-centeredness are broken down. They
record the moods and tempers of modern man, his distraught-
ness and malaise, his hidden longing for deliverance and redemption from the bondages of the soul. Modern man seeks a
way by which to walk, and gropes like the blind in search of a
wall of support. He goes hither and yon, seeking rest but find-
ing none. He is profoundly occupied with himself, and subjects
himself to infinite self-scrutiny. He feels himself kin with men
of other broken ages, whether the decline and fall of Assyria in
the seventh century B.C. when Jeremiah could cry, "Is there no
balm in Gilead? Is there no physician there?" (Jer. 8:22),[1] or
the decline and fall of Rome when Augustine wrote his *Confessions,* or the time of the French Revolution when Words-
worth complained that

> The world is too much with us; late and soon,
> Getting and spending, we lay waste our powers.

Modern man flees to the past, hoping to discover guidance
and direction for his confused and tortuous present, and returns to find that he is compelled to face the demands of his

[1] Scripture quotations are taken from the Revised Standard Version. The
few exceptions to this rule will be found on the following pages, where I
have used my own translation or made minor alterations in the RSV:
21, 23, 33, 37, 38, 42, 43, 48, 53, 55, 61, 71, 79, 115, 126.

own time. The children seek their lost fathers, and the fathers are disquieted by the aberrations and confusions of their sons. The young men rage in vain against a society which has lost its spiritual roots, and stage revolt against the conventions and mores of their elders. They "watch the dark fields for a rebirth of faith and wonder" where

> sounds no more the beat of the heart
> But only the sound of ultimate darkness falling
> And of blind Samson at the Fair, shaking the pillars
>   of the world and emptily calling.[2]

The times are out of joint, but the ethical dilemmas of our age are so many and so complex that the political leaders and statesmen are taxed to the limits of their capacities to set them right. The age of space has become the age of anxiety. We no longer look with much hope to the resolution of the gargantuan conflicts which rage throughout the earth or of the competing ideologies which stir the thoughts of men. The contemporary theater is as wide as the world is wide, and its temporal dimensions reach deep into our historic past. The questions of what we ought to do and what we ought not to do are always with us, and we now see that our choice is not simply between the absolute right and the absolute wrong. Yet we are always confronted with the necessity of reaching the best tolerable decisions.

The conviction which underlies the present discussion is that a way is offered contemporary man in his troubled "historicity" which may sustain him in his need, lead him to the peace for which he longs, and protect him from the demonic powers which seek to lay him low. It is the way of Israel. Matthew Arnold was fond of saying that it is this people which knows the way the world is going. It is true in a deeper sense than Arnold realized; yet his words gain their cogency when one enters into converse with this particular history, participates in its words and events, and commits oneself to the personal Lord of history of whom the Bible speaks. It is our intent, then, to describe the ethics and ethos of Israel, to trace the way she takes

[2] Edith Sitwell, "Invocation," in *The Collected Poems of Edith Sitwell* (New York: Vanguard Press, 1954).

in the time granted her by God, and, finally, to strike the highway that leads to her destination. In narrative and poetry her
words are spoken, and it is with these that we are called into
interior engagement.

When we venture to speak of the ethics of ancient Israel, we
are employing the term with considerable latitude. If by ethics
we mean the theory or science of right conduct, the principles
of morality, or the systematic analysis of "the good," then it is
clear that we shall look in vain in the pages of the Old Testament for such formulations. For here we find no unified and
coherent body of ethical principles, no autonomous values or
ideals which one can possess and make one's own, no norms
which have independent status in and of themselves. The Old
Testament contains no treatises on the nature of goodness,
truth, and justice. No Hebrew ever thought of writing a disser-
tation *de natura bonitatis* or *de natura veritatis*. The man of
Israel had no prior conception of goodness, no innate sense of
duty or right, no ideal of the virtuous life. This was not the
way of Israel's thinking. Rather, he knew that he had been
addressed, that he had been told what was required of him;
and he knew perfectly well when and where he had been told,
what the demands were which were incumbent upon him, and
Who it was Who had exacted of him such demands. He
knew perfectly well that he had not been confronted with
ethical abstractions, but rather had been addressed by One who
had spoken to him in the events of the great tradition of which
he was a part, to which he inwardly belonged, and which described him as a person.

What is good is what God requires; what is evil is what God
forbids. Yet this is not the manner of the divine speaking;
rather, God confronts his people with the basic imperative of
all biblical speech: *"Hear my voice!"* It is with the will and
word of God and indeed of a particular God—not the gods of
the nations—that man has to do, or rather, who has to do with
him. God for the ancient Israelite was not to be subordinated
to man's prior knowledge of what right is. When Abraham
pleaded in the great dialogue before the destruction of the cities
of the Plain, "Shall not the Judge of all the earth do right
(*mishpaṭ*)?" (Gen. 18:25), he could speak in this way because
the compiler of the ancient traditions knew of a time when

God had revealed his justice and right. For Israel, God is the eternally Prior One, who has entered into the midst of man's history to make his will and purpose known.

The Old Testament contains no definitions of ethical terminology. Words like truth, knowledge, justice, righteousness, and goodness have wide-ranging connotations in the original Hebrew which are often obscured in our modern renderings. We cannot simply assume that the English translation has the same associations as the original. Philological study may be of service to guide us in our understanding, but it is more often the context, the living relationship which words bear to one another, and the manner or convention of speaking, that will prove most rewarding and illuminating. The Old Testament is rich in ethical terminology, but it is striking that many of the words most congenial to modern man are absent. Such terms as morality, experience, conscience, personality, virtue, history, and nature are not to be found, although the reality they are designed to describe may *mutatis mutandis* be present.

Nevertheless, any attempt to translate the ancient Oriental, Semitic words into their Western equivalents inevitably involves the interpretation of the translator. Israelite thinking is notably practical, not theoretical and speculative. The most common and important verb for "to think" means to devise or to plan; thinking eventuates in activity. As a man thinks in his heart, so he is. It is not surprising, then, that the heart should be the seat both of thought and of will, for thought is related to the will. "All the Hebrew words most commonly used to designate the process of thinking reveal the movement of the soul in the direction of activity."[3] Hebrew thinking is dynamic, alive, full of movement. Knowledge is not understood abstractly or theoretically, but concretely and experientially. The verb "to know" is employed with great fluidity and versatility. It can mean to discern or to discriminate, but also to acknowledge and to hold in possession. More especially, it means to enter into interior relationship with, to have communion with. In this sense, to know good is to do it, to know one's sin is to confess and acknowledge it. It is to grasp a thing or person in its or his totality. Similarly, truth is not so much abstract or objective

[3] Johannes Pedersen, *Israel: Its Life and Culture* (London: Humphrey Milford, Oxford University Press, 1926) , I-II, p. 125.

as subjective and personal. It is something to be appropriated, that which is dependable, trustworthy, reliable, steadfast, and firm. To be true to a person is to be faithful to him, to be loyal to a relationship.

Memory plays an important role in Israel's way of thinking; the verb "to remember" means to activate into the living present, to actualize the past in such a way as to influence present decision and present conduct. The parts of the body are associated with psychical states; psychical states have a physical basis. This explains in part the numerous anthropomorphisms and anthropopathisms of the Old Testament. To be a person is to possess a body, but the body is more than a physical organism. The functioning of its organs often expresses not only the divine activity but also the intention which motivates the activity. Thus, the ways of the living God are understood realistically in relation to man's psychophysical life.

Objectivity and detachment are no Hebrew virtues. The Hebrew did not view life dispassionately. He did not seek to live in conformity to nature, to fulfill the law of his being, or to see life steadily and see it whole. He was not a philosopher. He did not seek to make reason prevail but the will of God, and he would not have thought of equating the two. The "flaw" in man did not lie in the intellect but in the will. His problem was not ignorance but disobedience, infidelity, and the obduracy of the heart. It was not a matter of being unable to think clearly but of living in accordance with the divine will and purpose. Human life must not conform to the laws of nature but to the Word of God, which was prior to and transcendent to nature, and, indeed, had brought the universe of nature into existence. The Israelite did not begin with certain a priori affirmations of reason but with a response of faith. He did not speculate about the First Cause, the arché or ratio of all things, but lived by the faith that the God who had delivered his people from bondage was the Creator of heaven and earth.

Creation was not an answer to speculative questions of cosmogony; it was the demonstration of the divine Lordship and sovereignty over history and nature. Creation is the prologue to a particular history; reflection upon it is derivative from God's action in history. History is the primary area of the divine revealing, and the universe of nature is subservient to it. The heavenly bodies were created that man might live in God's created time and by the Word addressed to him. The Israelite did not seek to escape the rhythmic cycle of recurring seasons, but listened to God's Word in particular times and occasions directing him to his destiny. The prophet, not the philosopher, is the most representative of what was distinctive in Israel. The prophet does not come with his own insight, his own intellectual acumen, his religious genius, the force of his personality, or his own moral rectitude, but as one who has been sent on a commission by an exalted and ruling King, who addresses himself to Israel in the concreteness and immediacy of a particular historical situation. There was no Academy or Stoa in Jerusalem, but rather the Temple where the sacred liturgies commemorating the eventful past were remembered and recited and celebrated, and where the events of the future were anticipated and made present in joyful songs of praise. There the Israelite heard the words of the Torah proclaimed, and acknowledged that he lived under an ultimate responsibility.

One of the best indices to an understanding of the ethos of a people is its way of speaking, the manner in which it uses words, its grammar and rhetoric. Much of the Old Testament was originally spoken, and the stamp of its original spokenness is deeply impressed upon it. This is why it gains so much by being read aloud. The ear can often grasp what the eye cannot; it is the ear, not the eye, that is the important organ in Israel's psychophysical imagery. Not only *what* is said is important but also *how* it is spoken—the ordering and disposition of the words, their stresses and nuances, where they begin and where they end. We shall be better prepared, then, to grasp the nature of Israel's cultural mentality and more particularly the nature of her sense of responsibility and obligation if we allow her to speak in her own way. Above all, we shall come to understand that the God in whom Israel found the source of her life and destiny was a speaking God and that Israel responded to his speaking in hearing and answering. In the pages of the Bible we listen to a God who is addressing, telling, recounting, informing, proclaiming, witnessing, exhorting, calling, admonishing, warning, teaching, and announcing. It is to a God who acts in these particular ways of speaking that Israel is called to respond. So we hear the people answering in many different ways according to the kinds of words that are spoken to it in a particular historical situation.

Vocatives play an important role in the speech of Israel. Yahweh *addresses* his people in many different ways and manners. He often addresses them with the second-person-singular pronoun, "thou," and in contexts where the urgency of obligation is pronounced. He addresses them with "O Israel," "O my people," "my chosen," "my servant," "faithless children," and with many similar vocatives. He often addresses them with more extended predications:

> O you who turn justice to wormwood,
>> and cast down righteousness to the earth!
>>>> Amos 5:7

> O afflicted one, storm-tossed, and not comforted.
>>>> Isaiah 54:11

To this speaking, Israel responds with all the rich terminology born of historical life: "O Yahweh," "O God of my right," "O Holy One of Israel," "O Shepherd of Israel," "my Rock and my Redeemer," "my King and my God," "O God of my salvation." In the speaking of these vocatives, Israel acknowledges the ultimate relationship in which she lives.

Yahweh has many *questions* to direct to his people. The first of all men listens to the awful words, "Where art thou?"; the first of all women, to that authentically biblical question, "What have you done?"; and the first son, to the unanswered question, "Where is your brother?" The oracles of the prophets fairly teem with the divine interrogatives. Jeremiah, the most inward of them all, is constantly confronting his people with the necessity of giving an answer. "What will you do when the end comes?" (Jer. 5:31). "Do you not fear me?" (Jer. 5:22). "Shall I not punish them for these things?" (Jer. 5:29). "How long will it be before you are made clean?" (Jer. 13:27b). Job has many questions to put to his friends:

> Will it be well with you when he searches you out?
>> Or can you deceive him, as one deceives a man?
>>>> Job 13:9

In the speech from the whirlwind, he is overwhelmed by an avalanche of words from the divine questioner. In the questions, Israel is reminded of her responsibility. In the questions, her ways are called into question.

Israel hears herself spoken to with many *commands* and *prohibitions*. In Deuteronomy, her life is constantly placed before the urgency of the divine command: "And now, O Israel, give heed!" "Keep my statutes and do them!" "Keep silence and hear!" "Choose life!" The prophets never weary of confronting Israel with the imperatives of God:

> Wash yourselves; make yourselves clean;
>   remove the evil of your doings
>   from before my eyes;
> cease to do evil,
>   learn to do good;
> seek justice,
>   correct oppression;
> defend the fatherless,
>   plead for the widow.
>
> Isaiah 1:16-17

Behind everything that Isaiah has to proclaim is the categorical imperative of all prophecy: "Hear the word of the Lord." This motif has its sources in the earliest traditions of Israel. Undergirding them all and from the earliest beginnings is the drive and power of the inescapable *du sollst.*

A rhetorical form especially characteristic of Israel's way of speaking is the *conditional sentence* with its protasis and apodosis. Israel faces the alternatives of the Either-Or, of hearing or not hearing, of obedience or disobedience, of faithful allegiance or rebellion. The conditional is an authentically biblical formulation. We hear it in the crucial context of the covenant event where the real issue is of becoming the people of God or of refusing to become his people (Exod. 19:5-6). We hear it when the twelve tribes enter for the first time into the covenant federation at Shechem (Josh. 24:14-15); the liturgy pulsates with the urgency of decision: *"Choose you this day whom you will serve"* (Josh. 24:15).

In the latter half of the seventh century B.C., when Assyria

was declining and Chaldea was rising to power, a time of international dislocation and ferment, Israel returns to the sources
of her life in the Mosaic age and listens again to the great conditionals, now elaborated both positively and negatively (Deut.
11:13-15, 22-25, 26-28; 28:1-6, 15-19). She is summoned to face
the supreme issue of her existence. The Either-Or is sounded
with great passion and eloquence; there is for her no *tertium
quid*. It is a matter of life or death, of a future or no future, of
the nature gods of the nations and the way of life of their
devotees *or* of the God of history, of the Exodus and Sinai, and
the way of life that he requires of the faithful. The two ways
are placed before her, of curse or blessing, of good or evil, of
obedience or disobedience, of life or death. The prophets never
weary of facing their people with the live alternatives; they,
too, preserve the conditionals, and it is clear whence they have
derived them:

> For if you truly amend your ways and your doings, if you
> truly execute justice one with another, if you do not oppress
> the alien, the fatherless or the widow, or shed innocent blood
> in this place, and if you do not go after other gods to your
> own hurt, then I will cause you to dwell in this place, in the
> land that I gave of old to your fathers for ever.
>   Jeremiah 7:5-7

We hear the same alternatives spoken in the royal hymns and
liturgies, especially in those where the covenant contexts are
most apparent (Pss. 89:30-34; 132:12). Wherever Israel stands
in the presence of her covenant Lord, there she is called to
render a decision.

Yahweh addresses his people in the first person. He speaks in
self-asseverations, which bring Israel into an immediate awareness of her life and destiny, of her obligation and accountability to a transcendent Other. The Subject addresses himself with
his first person "I" to the one whom he has chosen to be the
second-person "thou." He is speaking his own thoughts and in-
tentions. He is telling of himself by saying "I," and to the first
person subject he adds the live verbs of his activity for man.
The first words are spoken at the place of the covenant: "I am
Yahweh your God, who brought you out of the land of Egypt"
(Exod. 20:2). No words were better remembered in Israel,

none more frequently sounded in the precincts of the sanctuary. We hear them again and again in many different situations and in many different literary guises and forms, and with good reason, for in them Israel found the source and meaning of her life.

In the Holiness Code (Lev. 17-26), the divine first-person affirmations undergird all that is required of Israel. Statute follows upon statute, but they are established and given authority by the climactic word: *"I am Yahweh your God."* The repetitions are not merely stylistic; they are meant to call Israel to remembering and to hearing, to acknowledgment and to faith:

> You shall not hate your brother in your heart, but you shall reason with your neighbor, lest you bear sin because of him. You shall not take vengeance or bear a grudge against the sons of your own people, but you shall love your neighbor as yourself: *I am Yahweh.*
>
> Leviticus 19:17-18

Ezekiel brings many of his oracles to a climax with Yahweh's words for Israel's destiny: "Then you shall know that I am Yahweh." These self-asseverations reach their culmination in Second Isaiah; they appear profusely and in many different literary forms and patterns, but always it is the prophet's intention that his people should hear themselves addressed by the Lord of their future:

> I am Yahweh, your Holy One,
>   the Creator of Israel, your King.
>
> Isaiah 43:15

> I am Yahweh, and there is no other,
>   besides me there is no God.
>
> Isaiah 45:5a

The Old Testament portrays the mystery of the divine *pathos* in many stylistic modes and conventions of speech: reflective monologues, volitionals, optatives, ejaculations, apostrophes, among others. In them we seem to be peering into the mind and heart of God, for here he is exposing the feelings which stir him and the desires and hopes he has treasured within himself. He is moved with yearning and longing for Israel's return:

> O that my people would listen to me,
>   that Israel would walk in my ways!
>
> Psalm 81:13; cf. Isaiah 48:18

There was the hour of the covenant when Israel had committed herself:

> Oh that they had such a mind as this always, to fear me and to keep all my commandments, that it might go well with them and with their children for ever!
>
> Deuteronomy 5:29

God's patience is sometimes at an end, so he vents the fury of his terrible wrath upon them:

> The Lord goes forth like a mighty man,
>   like a man of war he stirs up his fury;
> he cries out, he shouts aloud,
>   he shows himself mighty against his foes.
>
> Isaiah 42:13; cf. 57:11

But there is also conflict within him, between the justice that demands and the grace that conquers the demands of justice:

> How can I give you up, O Ephraim!
>   How can I surrender you, O Israel!
> How can I make you like Admah!
>   How can I treat you like Zeboim!
> My heart recoils within me,
>   my compassion grows warm and tender.
> I will not execute my fierce anger,
>   I will not again destroy Ephraim;
> for I am God and not man,
>   the Holy One in your midst,
>   and I will not come to destroy.
>
> Hosea 11:8-9; cf. 14:8;
> Micah 6:3, 5; Matthew 23:27

We are listening to the laments of God. We hear him telling of
his grief and pain because of the infidelity and self-will of his
people. In a bold anthropomorphism, Yahweh rises up early
to send his servants the prophets to call Israel to repentance, so
anxious is he that they return (Jer. 7:13, 25; 11:7; 25:4). Such
passages as these reflect as no others all that evil does to God, all
the suffering it entails, all that man's offense to man ultimately
means. There is the answering *pathos* of Israel. We listen to
her weeping and her broken cries of contrition and remorse.
She, too, knows the interior volitional of the "O that . . ." (Isa.
64:1 ff.; cf. Jer. 14:8 ff., 19 ff.; Pss. 77:1 ff.; 89:46 ff.). In Lamen-
tations the *pathos* of Israel moves into a mighty crescendo.
Here Israel has found words for her deepest griefs.

The cultural mentality of a people is reflected not only in its
rhetoric but also in the literary types and patterns of speech in
which it expresses itself most congenially and naturally. We
turn, therefore, to some of the most characteristic ways of
Israel's speaking, especially as they relate to the nature of the
demand laid upon her.

1. *Narrative.* The most representative and characteristic
mode of biblical speech is narrative. It is completely centered
in action and movement. Beginning and end are always kept
firmly in mind. Everything proceeds from the opening sentence
and presses forward in action to the outcome. The verbs hold a
position of central importance in Hebrew narration; they give
action and vitality to it, and their grammatical forms are such
as to present a continuous, unbroken flow of movement. Everything contributes to the telling of the event; nothing must im-
pede the course of its action, neither setting nor description nor
portraiture nor psychological analysis. The narrative, like the
poem, is relatively short and compressed. Emphasis is given by
repetition. Character is indicated by action. There are no
heroes in the Greek or modern sense of the word; heroic stature
is always subordinated to the overarching purpose and sovereignty of God and is qualified by human frailty and pride.
The individual narratives are gathered into large literary
complexes, and these in turn into still more spacious units until
the narrative extends from creation to the end of the monarchy, and theologically beyond that to the consummation at
the end of days. Old Testament narrative is of many forms and

varieties. It rises to its greatest height in the history of David's reign (II Sam. 9-20; I Kings 1-2), unsurpassed in the literatures of antiquity, but here too the narrative is dominated by a single motif from beginning to end, the activity of the Spirit and the realization of the divine intention in history. Israel has a story to tell to the world. It is a recounting of God's ways with man and of man's response in obedience or rebellion. "The Hebrews took the significance of historical action so seriously that they were driven toward an absolute, all-embracing historical view of man and the world."[4]

2. *Law.* The translation of the Hebrew word "Torah" as "law" is not felicitous and has unfortunately been responsible for much misunderstanding by those who misinterpret its meaning and exaggerate the legalism of ancient Israel. Rather, we should render the word in the majority of cases, surely in the pre-exilic period, as instruction or teaching. Often it is tantamount to revelation and is indeed referred to as God's Word. The Torah has the highest authority because it is given by God as an expression of his will for his people. While it was pre-eminently the function of the priest "to handle the Torah," it was by no means confined to him, for prophets (I Sam. 12:23; Isa. 1:10), sages (Job 6:24), and elders (cf. Deut. 31:9) also gave instruction to the people.

The legal literature contains numerous corpora of teaching. Some of them appear as pentads, others as decalogues, others as dodecalogues. The individual demands are of many types and varieties. Similar in form and sometimes in content to the formulations of the other peoples of the ancient Near East are the casuistic or case laws in the If-then style: "If you lend money to any of my people with you who is poor, you shall not be to him a creditor, and you shall not exact interest from him" (Exod. 22:25).

Most characteristic of Israel's legal teaching, however, is the categorical formulation, *thou shalt not:* "Thou shalt not bear witness against thy neighbor" (Exod. 20:16). Sometimes this apodictic form appears in the participial style: "Whoever curses his father and mother shall be put to death" (Exod. 21:15). Still another form opens with "the man who": "A man or a

---

[4] Tom F. Driver, *The Sense of History in Greek and Shakespearean Drama* (New York: Columbia University Press, 1960), pp. 47-48.

woman who is a medium or a wizard shall be put to death"
(Lev. 20:27). The curse is still another form of the apodictic
teaching: "Cursed be he who misleads a blind man on the
road" (Deut. 27:18). In Deuteronomy, the laws often appear in
homiletical contexts; it is proclaimed, or preached law (Deut.
15:1-18). The Torah was proclaimed in the Temple by priest
or cultic prophet, notably at the Feast of Tabernacles or at the
New Year. Thither the people repaired to hear the words
spoken to them. The purpose of such occasions was to teach the
people and thus to effect a change in their behavior.

3. *Blessing and curse.* While these are fixed stylistic forms,
they undergo transformation in the course of Israel's history.
The purpose of the blessing is to confer favor, prosperity, peace,
security, and posterity upon the one who is blessed. It is significant that while the blessing is frequently associated with
Yahweh, the curse is seldom or never directly ascribed to him.
At the same time, the curses in Deuteronomy 27:15-26 were
originally associated with the center of the amphictyony at
Shechem, and they held a place of importance in the amphic-
tyonic cult there. In the Psalter, we receive a clear picture of
who are blessed and what the nature of the blessing is. He is
blessed (or happy) who obeys Yahweh's law (Ps. 1:1-3), for he
has living resources, like a tree planted by channels of water,
and whatever he does prospers (cf. Jer. 17:7-8). All who take
refuge in Yahweh are blessed (Ps. 2:11c), all who have been
forgiven (Ps. 32:1), who trust in Yahweh (Ps. 40:4a), who consider the poor or weak (Ps. 41:1), who find their strength in
God (Ps. 84:5), who dwell in the Temple, "ever singing thy
praise" (Ps. 84:4). That nation is blessed which has Yahweh
for its God (Ps. 33:12).

4. *Invective and threat.* The prophets of Israel were heirs to
the revealed law. Sometimes we hear echoes from the decalogues (Hos. 4:2; Jer. 7:9), at other times they give their own
Torah (Amos 4:4-5; 5:4-5, 21-24; Isa. 1:10-17). Disobedience to
the will of God means divine judgment, which is classically
formulated in the invective and threat. These are the most
characteristic of the prophetic ways of speaking. They appear
more frequently than any other literary forms and are employed with great versatility. The classical form of the invective
opens with "woe to," whereas the threat begins with the em-

phatic and decisive "therefore." They are often introduced with
the salutation of the royal messenger, "thus says the Lord," and
are concluded with "says the Lord" or "oracle of the Lord."
The first two chapters of Amos preserve the invective and
threat in almost perfect form; in Hosea, they seem to have been
disturbed. More elaborate formulations appear in Isaiah (e.g.,
Isa. 5:8 ff.) . Ezekiel employs the classical "woe" and "therefore"
style, but he often transforms it into the "because" and "therefore" (Ezek. 13:2b-15; 25:3b-7, 8-11) .

5. *Exhortation*. Nowhere is this form represented with
greater eloquence than in Deuteronomy. It is the most stirring
prose in the Old Testament. Not only are the laws framed in
the context of preaching, but there are whole chapters which
are hortatory pleas for obedience, and the pleas are constantly
associated with life: "Give heed to the statutes and the ordinances . . . that you may live" (Deut. 4:1). The opening speech
of Moses extending through four long chapters comes to a climax of almost overwhelming power (Deut. 4:32-40), and what
makes it particularly gripping is that it appears after the long
survey of Israel's past. Exhortation to obedience is grounded in
the history which is a manifestation of grace and love. This is
preaching: admonition and warning and pleading. The
prophets resort to this same literary form upon occasion, as do
the psalmists, especially in covenantal contexts (Pss. 50:7 ff.;
81:8 ff.) .

6. *Liturgy*. In the liturgy, Israel enters into an engagement
of holy speaking and holy hearing. She participates in sacred
dialogue with the God of her history. She hears herself addressed by priest or cultic prophet, and then gives the answer
that is required of her. The origin of this form is to be seen perhaps in the early antiphonals, such as the Song of Miriam in the
hour of the great deliverance (Exod. 15:20-21) . These elemental forms were destined to be elaborated, as in the superb
liturgy of Psalm 136. The liturgies are of many different forms
and styles and are designed for many different occasions, above
all for the commemorations at the festivals of the *magnalia Dei*.
Israel is taking to herself the words and deeds of Yahweh and is
giving the confessional response which his words and deeds by
their very nature required.

7. *Confession*. The devout Israelite exposed the depths of his

heart in dialogical encounters with his God. He poured out his anxieties and fears and despairs to him who searches the heart of man and listens to the words of his lips. The most familiar of these self-disclosures are found in Jeremiah (11:18-12:6; 15:10-21; 17:8-10, 14-18; 18:18-23; 20:7-18), but they are also present in the Psalter (Pss. 51, 139), in Second Isaiah (50:4-9; 53:1-9), and elsewhere. Seldom is the existential mentality of the Israelite more clearly revealed than here. He confesses that he has done what he ought not to have done. Any claim that he has done what he ought to have done receives little encouragement (Jer. 15:19-21; 12:5-6).

8. *Wisdom*. The wise man's ways of speaking are extremely varied and rich. They range from the simplicity of the maxim, aphorism, or proverb to the essaylike reflections of Qoheleth to the dramatic dialogue of Job. The sage is fond of contrasting the conduct of the good man with that of the evil man in antithetic parallelism (Prov. 10:1-2; 12:1-8, 17-28). One way of behavior is better than another; it is better to do *this* than *that* (Prov. 16:19; 25-7). In many other ways, he tells us what is better and what is worse (Prov. 12:9; 15:16f.; 16:19; 27:4; 28:6). Even more simply he tells us that "it is not good" to do certain things (Prov. 25:27, etc.). He is fond of calling his pupils to hear what he has to teach them (Prov. 1:8-9; 4:1-2, 20-22; 7:24-27) and he explains why.

Then there are the strict prohibitions: "do not" (Prov. 3:25-32; 6:30), and to them the sage adds the consequences of right or wrong conduct. Wisdom is rich in similitudes (Prov. 25:11-14, 25-26; 26:7-11) and little parables (Prov. 6:6-11; 9:1-6). Occasionally we come upon autobiographical vignettes (Prov. 4:3-9), but more frequently upon elaborate hypotactic constructions (Prov. 1:10-18; 2:1-22). In this literature we are told succinctly, if not always profoundly, what the good life is like. The mood pervading much of it is that of the conscientious and dedicated teacher.

9. *Apology*. There were times when the man of Israel had to take a stand in defense of himself, when the situation demanded that he make no concession or compromise, when he was compelled to speak out and bear the consequences. "Come what may, this I will say and not retract!" Like Martin Luther he is saying, "Here I stand, I can do no other." The

issue must be drawn, the alternatives stated, the decision made, fearlessly and unequivocally. Amos speaks such words of defense to Amaziah, priest of Bethel (Amos 7:14-15), and adds to them the characteristically biblical "now therefore" (Amos 7:16-17). Over against the optimistic prophets of his time who facilely cried *Shalom,* and profited from their trade, Micah delivers his succinct and incorruptible *apologia,* "as for me" (Mic. 3:8). It is not an *apologia pro vita sua* that we have here so much as a defense of the divine calling and commission: "Yahweh sent me!" One of the most remarkable "oaths of clearance" is made by Job (Job 31). It is a noble utterance of unclouded vision, of honor and integrity, in a way quite *sui generis* in the whole of Scripture; nor is it a merely humanistic defense of the good life. If he had not behaved as he did, he "could not have faced his majesty," he would "have been false to God above" (Job 31:23b, 28b).

Our examination of the ways of Israel's speaking yields certain conclusions of the first importance for our understanding of biblical ethics and more particularly of the manner of Israel's life:

1. There are numerous different ways in which words are ordered into forms and types; we have selected only a few of the most representative of these. Within each type there is a strong sense of form and structure and a terminology characteristic of the type; at the same time there is great variety and fluidity within each so that no form ever becomes a mere stereotype.

2. While we have spoken of the *literary* character of the forms, the literary interest as such is never cultivated; the Israelite did not compose his compositions for aesthetic purposes. The forms were determined by convention and custom. *This was the way one spoke on this occasion.*

3. In all the forms we have studied we are listening to words *spoken.* It is the manner of Israel to speak in many ways and fashions. Israel is called to an oral engagement, to participation in the responsibility of the give-and-take of words.

4. Through all the forms we sense Israel's awareness that she is *accountable,* accountable to the transcendent Lord. God is the supremely relevant Subject within and behind her ex-

istence. Israel knows that her origins are with him and that her destiny is with him. That is the meaning of Torah. Always she is called to choice and decision.

5. The study of forms must not be isolated from the historical and theological contexts in which they exist. We must inquire not only into the general kind of situation in which the particular way of speaking was employed but, so far as it is possible, into the precise occasion which evoked such speaking.

2
The Symbols of the Way

THE PROHIBITION AGAINST THE MAKING OF IDOLS
and the general resistance to spatial imagery exercised a pro-
found influence upon the mentality of ancient Israel and the
way of her life. It is reflected, for example, in the general absence of visualizing descriptions in most of the Old Testament,
in the general recession of the world of seeing to the world of
hearing, and perhaps, too, in the paucity of the use of adjec-
tives. It is all the more remarkable, therefore, that the language of Israel should abound in figurative speech of many
kinds, with symbolisms of varying range and intensity, and
above all with anthropomorphisms and anthropopathisms in
which the parts of the body with their psychical associations
are ascribed to God. Similes, metaphors, metonomies, synec-
doches, personifications, parables, allegories, and myths are
employed to body forth the nature of the responsible relationship which Israel bears to the Determiner of her destiny.
A study of the kind of symbols employed and of the functions
they serve would therefore prove rewarding for our grasp of
biblical mentality, but it is our intention at this point to de-
lineate some of the major areas of symbolic discourse which
portray the meaning, nature, and dynamic of the divine imperative and demand.

The first of these centers about the power of the spoken
word. The word (*dabar*) is the most elemental form of speech.
In Hebrew, it has many meanings and connotations. It can
mean thing and event as well as word; word and event, indeed,
have an interior association. Thus the word *happens,* and in
the event the word is spoken. The *dabar* is alive because it is
born within the self of the speaker, and bears within it the
vitality and power of the speaker. The word becomes alive in
its speaking; it initiates dialogue, invites response, calls to

action, and registers its effect upon the one addressed by the uniqueness of the spoken name. The Named One addresses the one who also bears a name. The *dabar* contains the will and intention of the speaker. The will is made concrete and present in the immediacy of the Word spoken. It is through the word that the speaker extends himself, as far as the word is heard and remembered. It is not merely the influence of the personality of the speaker but rather the power of the spoken word of the particular speaker that is important. Thus the word has a direction, a goal, and a destiny. Through the word the event is grasped and appropriated. The word has both noetic content and dynamic force, the content of knowledge and the power and drive of the speaking self. The self meets the other self in the word spoken. Time is appropriated in hearing. The word is pre-eminently the symbol for action in time. That God should speak is a matter of supreme consequence. His Word determines the course that Israel is to pursue in history.

In the theophanies, the *hieros logos* is spoken, and the sanctuaries preserve the memory of the event by the words that are recited and sung in the great celebrations. Worship brings into present awareness and present event the words that were once spoken in the memorable events of the past, supremely, of course, the holy Name, Yahweh. Words are made present by being spoken. It is the function of the cult to bring past events and future events into the immediacy of the present hour by the vitality of the spoken words. The words of the prophet are remembered by his disciples, the counsels of the sage by his pupils, the torah of the priest by the devotees.

The elemental character and power of the word is revealed in the brevity of many Hebrew literary forms, as in the pregnant succinctness of the commands (*debarim*). Yahweh's will was communicated by the ten words (Exod. 20:1-17). The invectives and threats of the prophets are also "words," and Yahweh's call to them is the coming of his Word: "the Word of the Lord came [happened] to me." Yahweh's Word determines the movement of history, from the Word to Abraham (Gen. 12:1-3) to its fulfillment, from the Word to David (II Sam. 7) to it fulfillment, from the words of the prophets to their fulfillment (I-II Kings). With his Word history begins,

and it is so powerful that it will accomplish its purpose in the
world:

> For as the rain comes down,
>   and the snow from heaven,
> and thither does not return,
>   except it water the earth,
> and make it bring forth and sprout,
>   and gives seed to the sower,
>   and bread to the eater,
> so shall my word be
>   which goes forth from my mouth,
>   and it shall not return to me empty,
> but it shall accomplish that which I purpose,
>   and prosper in the thing for which I sent it.
>
> Isaiah 55:10-11

The political, social, and international orders are under the
rule of the divine Word as is the destiny of Israel and the
nations. Thus the prophets join with the lawgivers in their
summons, "Hear, O Israel." *What is required of Israel is spoken
to her.* If Yahweh has a word to speak, he sends his servants the
prophets to proclaim it.

The primary image to express conduct or behavior in the
Old Testament is the "way" or "road" (*derek*) . No other image
was more rich and manifold, none more diverse in nuance and
connotation. The Hebrew words for road can be translated in
a number of different ways, but it is the verbs of action associated with them that best reveal the versatility of usage and
the dynamic character of the symbol, above all the verb "to
walk" or "to go" and, indeed, the many different kinds of going
and walking. The way of a man was the course he followed
through life, the direction of his going, and the manner of his
walking. It was a good word because it was drawn from the
vicissitudes of daily life, from a land of many roads and paths
in which walking was the usual manner of going from one place
to another. It was a good symbol because it involved beginning and end and the intention which prompted the journey.
There were different ways a man might take, and his journey
involved decision or choice of the right or the wrong road.

It was admirably suited as an expression for historical existence, for the life lived in time and event, and for the movement and action of the life lived on the road. Here again we
may observe the psychophysical character of Israel's way of
thinking, for walking or going was more than a merely physical undertaking; it involved the purpose for which the journey
was taken. It was always a *particular* walking because the content of the intention was always particular.

What makes this terminology of supreme importance in
Israel's manner of thinking is that it is applied to God. He is
Israel's Leader, who goes on before (Deut. 1:30, 33; Ps. 68:7),
as a shepherd before his flock (Ps. 77:20), and shows her the
path of life (Ps. 16:11). All his paths are steadfast love and
faithfulness to those who keep covenant (Ps. 25:10). The symbol was employed as a major expression not only of biblical
ethics but also of providence, piety, history, and eschatology.
To walk the way God commanded was to walk the right way
and to move in the right direction; to walk with him was to be
devout (Gen. 5:22); to follow his leading was to be faithful
and loyal and to move forward toward the goal or destination.
In eschatological time, Israel is called to fulfill her mission in
the world to prepare the way of the Lord (Isa. 40:3).

A man's way and a man's deed are one and the same. The
way in which he ought to walk and what he ought to do are
synonymous (Exod. 18:20; Jer. 7:3, 5), and it is characteristic
of the Old Testament that the deeds are specified. Obedience
is walking in the way of the commandments of God (Deut.
5:32 and often); disobedience is turning aside from it (Exod.
32:8; Deut. 9:12, 16; 11:28). The divine requirements or commands are the divine ways (Deut. 8:6; Ps. 119:15). This terminology of the way is clearly a covenantal way of speaking.

> But this command I gave them, "Obey my voice, and I will
> be your God, and you shall be my people; and walk in all
> the way that I command you, that it may be well with you."
> Jeremiah 7:23

It is God who determines the right way; it is he who points
the way a man should go. Without his leading, Israel does not
know the way to take. She is always confronted with the choice
between the good road and the bad, the straight road and the
crooked. The good road is the way of life and well-being:

Thou dost show me the path of life;
   in thy presence there is fullness of joy,
   in thy right hand are pleasures for evermore.
                            Psalm 16:11

But the wrong road leads to death:

In the path of righteousness is life,
   but the way of error leads to death.
                         Proverbs 12:28

Many are they who stumble on the road:

But the path of the righteous is like the light of dawn,
   which shines brighter and brighter until full day.
The way of the wicked is like deep darkness;
   they do not know over what they stumble.
                     Proverbs 4:18-19

So men are called to choose between the two ways:

Thus says the Lord:
"Stand by the roads, and look,
   and ask for the ancient paths,
where the good way is; and walk in it,
   and find rest for yourselves."
                      Jeremiah 6:16

The alternatives are eloquently proclaimed in the great exhortation:

See, I have set before you this day life and good, death
and evil. If you obey the commandments of the Lord your
God, which I command you this day, by loving the Lord
your God, by walking in his ways, . . . then you shall live
and multiply, and the Lord your God will bless you. . . .
But if your heart turns away, and you will not hear, . . .
I declare to you this day, that you will perish. . . . Therefore, choose life, that you and your descendants may live.
                     Deuteronomy 30:15-19

So the pious suppliant calls upon God to lead his steps in the
right way:

Make me to know thy ways, O Lord;
　teach me thy paths,
Lead me in thy truth, and teach me,
　for thou art the God of my salvation;
　for thee I wait all the day long.

Psalm 25:4

The whole sphere of justice, particularly as it was implemented in the institution of the court of law, proved to be a major source of Israel's ethical terminology and imagery. It was before the judges, particularly the elders representing the leading families of the locality, that the individual found himself faced with his responsibility as a member of the community of Israel, where he was called to account for what he had done and where he was required to give answer. There he was declared innocent (*ṣaddīk*) or guilty (*rash'a*), in the right or in the wrong. In the Covenant Code (Exod. 21-23) we have an ancient transcript of some of the decisions (*mishpatīm*) of the judges at the city gate (Exod. 21:2-22:16). It is noteworthy that these judgments, similar in form and to some extent in content to the laws of other ancient Near Eastern formulations as they are, have been completely absorbed into the characteristically Israelite apodictic laws with their absolute and uncompromising "thou shall not." The case laws were originally secular in character, but their context makes them something quite different, for they were placed at Sinai, in the hour of the covenant, as Yahweh's ordinances to his people.

It is not so much with the Israelite court of law that we are concerned here, but rather with the fundamental consideration that the whole sphere of justice is drawn into the divine economy. In Israel, it is God who is the Judge, the final and ultimate Arbiter. It is he who dispenses justice and gives the laws to Israel for her instruction and guidance. He is the Protector and Establisher of the right. This motif is already found in our earliest literary strata, as is illustrated by the ancient formula, "May Yahweh judge between you and me" (Gen. 16:5; I Sam. 24:15; cf. Gen. 31:53), and persists throughout the whole Old Testament. The lines from an ancient liturgy incorporated in Isaiah express succinctly Israel's confession about her God:

For the Lord is our Judge, the Lord is our Ruler,
the Lord is our King; he will save us.

Isaiah 33:22

As Israel's King, the Lord is also Judge. As sovereign over
her existence, he determines what is right and what is wrong.
His will is the supreme issue for her life, exalted above the
wills of human judges and leaders. But more than that, while
his function is to maintain justice, to uphold the right, to
preserve the peace and well-being of the community, it is not
his punitive judgment that is central in the legal contexts but
rather his desire to protect the right and to establish it, to help
and to save Israel, to come to the rescue of those who have no
voice in court. Therefore, as Judge he is the Helper and Savior
and Deliverer and Redeemer of his people.

Yahweh's judicial role is illustrated in the many lawsuits in
which he appears both as Judge and as Plaintiff (Isa. 1:2-3;
1:18-20; 3:13-15; Jer. 2:2-13; Hos. 4:1-3; Mic. 6:1-8; Pss. 50,
82, 96-98; Isa. 41:1-42:4; 43:8-13; 45:20-24; 48:15-16; 50:8-9;
Dan. 6:13 ff.). The Lord takes his stand to judge his people,
and he has an indictment (*ribh*) against them:

> The Lord has taken his place to contend,
>   he stands to judge his people.
> The Lord enters into judgment
>   with the elders and princes of his people:
> "It is you who have devoured the vineyard,
>   the spoil of the poor is in your houses.
> What do you mean by crushing my people,
>   by grinding the face of the poor?"
>   says the Lord God of hosts.
>
> Isaiah 3:13-16

Micah 6:1-8 gives the lawsuit in more developed form and
preserves the dialogical encounter, a characteristic feature of
the lawsuits at the gate, between Judge and litigant. First, the
summons to hearing:

> Hear what the Lord is saying!
>
> Micah 6:1a

Then the appeal to present the case before the mountains and hills, who serve as witnesses to the dispute:

> Hear, you mountains, the controversy of the Lord,
>   and you enduring foundations of the earth;
> for the Lord has a controversy with his people,
>   and he will contend with Israel.
>
> Micah 6:2

Then follows the indictment of the Judge with its address and the questions he has to direct to the litigant:

> O my people, what have I done to you?
>   In what have I wearied you? Answer me!
>
> Micah 6:3

The Judge recounts the saving acts which had made Israel the people it was and calls it to remember them. The litigant replies with words of contrition:

> With what shall I come before the Lord,
>   and bow myself before God on high?
>
> Micah 6:6a

The prophet speaking as plaintiff has the last word:

> You have been told, O man, what is good;
>   and what does the Lord require of you,
> but to do justice, and to love steadfast love,
>   and to walk humbly with your God.
>
> Micah 6:8

This is genuinely biblical speaking and hearing. We hear it again in many other judicial encounters. It is clear that Israel's Judge is protecting the right and seeking to establish it. If we speak of the way of Israel, it is to contexts such as these that we do well to go. Israel's destiny is under judgment of a transcendent holy will.

Another of the ways of speaking by which Israel seeks to give expression to what is required of man is drawn from the life that is lived within the family. The family is the most elemental expression of community in ancient Israel, the most cohesive of the bonds which unite men, the community of those who share a common life. The unity of the family is centered in the father. He is at once its creator, its head, its master, the source of its life and blessing. He represents the family not only in legal matters but in cultic as well, for he stands at the head of it. He is the redeemer of the children who have been sold to slavery. The relationship of the father to his family is not merely physical; it is psychical and "spiritual" as well. The physical relationship is the bearer of the psychical. All of this suggests that family terminology was suited for an expression of the relationship between God and people, and especially for the nature of the relationship which united them.

The bond which unites Israel into a community is that all its members have one Father; this means, in the thought of Israel, that they share a common obligation and responsibility to the ultimate source of their life and history:

> Have we not all one father?
> Has not one God created us?
> Why then are we faithless to one another,
>   profaning the covenant of our fathers?
>   Malachi 2:10

In the bond of the family all Israelites are one, and all are called to filial obedience and faithfulness. But there is more here. They are united not only in the bond of their common creation but also in the bond of the covenant which was the goal of creation. As Father, God requires obedience of his sons. The motif appears again and again in the Old Testament:

> Hear, O heavens, and give ear, O earth;
>   for the Lord has spoken:
> "Sons have I reared and brought up,
>   but they have rebelled against me.
> The ox knows its owner,
>   and the ass its master's crib,
> but Israel does not know,
>   my people does not understand."
>   Isaiah 1:2-3

The first intention of God was that his people should be his sons (Exod. 4:22-23; Hos. 11:1-9; Jer. 3:19), but they were not true sons because they did not live in accordance with the will of the Father.

All Israelites are *brothers* and are therefore under obligation to each other. It is a wonderful thing for brothers to dwell together in unity, very good and pleasant (Ps. 133:1). The social legislation of Deuteronomy keeps reminding Israel of the demands that brotherhood makes upon them. "Remember that he is your brother." Even the Edomite must not be abhorred, "for he is your brother" (Deut. 23:7). Frequently, of course, the term is used almost as a convention (as it is in the Near East today), but often it is not so. In one of the oracles to the nations in Amos, Tyre is castigated because it "did not remember the covenant of brothers," and the brother here is not Israel but Edom (Amos 1:9)!

Another of the family relationships used to characterize Israel's understanding of her relationship to God was that of husband and bride. It is noteworthy that neither here nor in the father-son relationship is there any suggestion of a physical union, as among the other religions of the ancient Near East. The bonds which unite Yahweh the Husband and Israel the Bride are devotion, fidelity, justice, and that interior knowledge which comes from mutual respect, fidelity, and love.

Finally, the ethical terminology of Israel is not infrequently drawn from the sphere of education or teaching. This is most apparent in the Wisdom literature, but it is by no means confined to it. It is abundant in the legal and prophetic literature as well. The parents were the first teachers of the child, and it is their function to instruct him in the ways of the fathers. The ancient traditions must be remembered and passed on to succeeding generations. The practices and mores of the community must be perpetuated, and the obligations of the individual to the social group as a whole must be constantly repeated so that the group's solidarity and cohesiveness may be maintained and established. So when the child inquired why certain obligations were incumbent upon him, the parents had to have a ready answer.

We are well-informed as to the nature of the instruction. First of all, the traditions of course, but these included the narration of the mighty acts and an affirmation of the obligations which followed from them. The *magnalia* not only explained why it was that Israel was so different from other peoples in the world; they were also the source of her responsibilities. It belongs to the ethos of ancient Israel that every person be schooled in the unique traditions of the past and in the responsibilities associated with them. One could not listen to the old stories, laws, and songs without realizing that he himself was involved in them, that they belonged to him as a man in Israel. This was an essential part of a man's training and discipline. Discipline is moral direction, correction, and chastening. The *Shema* is perhaps the best statement in the whole Old Testament of the obligations of the Israelite to his children:

> Hear, O Israel! The Lord our God is one Lord; and you shall love the Lord your God with all your heart, and with all your life [*nephesh*], and with all your might. And these words which I command you this day shall be upon your heart, and you shall teach them diligently to your children, and shall talk of them when you sit in your house, and when you walk by the way, and when you lie down, and when you rise. And you shall bind them as a sign upon your hand, and they shall be as frontlets between your eyes. And you shall write them on the doorposts of your house and on your gates.
>
> Deuteronomy 6:4-9

It is well to be reminded again that the early traditions were transmitted orally. They were spoken, and they were remembered.

Yahweh is the Teacher of Israel. It is he who teaches Israel the course her life should take. In a very early source he assures Moses that he will be "with his mouth" and will teach him what he shall speak to Pharaoh (Exod. 4:12, 15). He gives the law to Moses for the instruction of Israel (Exod. 24:12). So he addresses his people:

> I will instruct you and teach you
> in the way you should go,
>
> Psalm 32:8

and the devotee can respond:

> Good and upright is the Lord;
>> therefore he instructs sinners in the way,
>>> Psalm 25:8

and the suppliant constantly pleads:

> Teach me thy statutes.
>> Psalm 119:26b; also
>> vss. 64, 68, 108, 124

It was the priests and Levites above all others to whom the teaching traditions were entrusted (Deut. 17:8-11; Lev. 10:11). In the Blessing of Moses, the latter are given their commission:

> They shall teach Jacob thy ordinances,
>> and Israel thy law.
>>> Deuteronomy 33:10

Prophets also perpetuated the ancient teachings; indeed, the prophetic proclamation has not infrequent affinities with the divine *toroth*. One of the most frequent plaints of Jeremiah is that Israel would not listen to the divine teaching (Jer. 17:23; 32:33; 35:13b). Zephaniah diagnoses the guilt of Israel in similar fashion:

> She listens to no voice,
>> she will not accept discipline.
>>> Zephaniah 3:2a

The interior relation between Teacher and taught, the Teaching One and the learning one, is superbly expressed in the words of the Servant of the Lord:

> The Lord God has given me
>> the tongue of those who are taught,
> that I may know how to sustain with a word
>> him that is weary.
> Morning by morning he wakens,
>> he wakens my ear
>> to hear as those who are taught.
>>> Isaiah 50:4

The Teacher of Israel is not an academician. He lives in intimate relationship with those who require to be taught. Thus the faithful Israelite can say that *"he causes me to know, he causes me to hear, he causes me to learn."* It is the way of the God of Israel to transform men's declarative (the *qal* stem) into the divine causative (the *hiph 'il* stem). It was Jeremiah who had to learn that again and again, as did the psalmists of Israel and the Apostle Paul in the New Testament. The Teacher is generous with his instructions and counsels and admonitions. For these, Israel rejoices and is thankful.

> Open my eyes, that I may behold
>   wondrous things out of thy teaching.
>
> Psalm 119:18

> Oh, how I love thy teaching!
>   It is my meditation all the day.
>
> Psalm 119:97

The penitent pleading for forgiveness strikes the same note:

> Then I will teach transgressors thy ways,
>   and sinners will return to thee.
>
> Psalm 51:13

In the new age of great compassion and everlasting love all the sons of Israel will be taught by the Lord (Isa. 54:7, 8, 13; cf. Jer. 31:33).

There are other ways in which the divine sovereignty and jurisdiction over Israel's historical life is expressed in the Old Testament. There is, above all, the rich terminology associated with the kingship of God, the dominating and overarching reality of all biblical faith, to which all other motifs and categories are subordinate. There is also the spacious ideology of redemption with its imagery drawn from the institution of slavery. It is significant that it was this imagery that came to dominate others in later reflection upon Yahweh's great deliverance of his people, and it in turn was employed to describe the eschatological event of forgiveness and deliverance.

3
The Beginning of the Way

THE WAY OF ISRAEL IS HISTORICAL. IT IS HISTORI-
cal to a maximum degree because its history belongs to God.
History is God's gift to Israel and to the world. It is a unique
gift, not only because events and times are unique, but also
because of the particular nature of these unique events and
times. Israel's career in the world has its beginning in the
divine initiative in a particular event. The event is God's
event for Israel. It is with reference to that event that Israel
comprehends her existence. It is meant for Israel's present,
but more than that it determines the course her future is to
take. The event is to be appropriated as the reality which
belongs to Israel, makes her the people of history in a unique
sense, and protects her from meaninglessness throughout the
course of the centuries which follow. The event is God's Word;
in it, God is speaking to Israel and to the world. So powerful
is his Word, so alive in the life that his Word has, that it opens
the way to the future and becomes the guiding force to determine the way Israel is to take. Without the Word spoken,
there would be no history, for it would be without the meaning and direction which his Word gives to it. The Word attends history, accompanies it in its tortuous movement, and
is spoken in concrete times by those who are sent by God to
proclaim it. The Word is revelation in history and for history.

The historical character of the way of Israel is revealed in
the words which God speaks to Moses when Moses inquires
about God's name (Exod. 3:13). The divine reply has usually
been rendered, "I am who I am," but this is surely an in-
felicitous translation of the Hebrew. The vocalization of the
verb was very probably originally causative. It means first of
all "to happen" or "to come to pass," and this is the meaning
required here: "I cause to happen what happens." This is of

course the whole issue of the great colloquy. God will bring to effect what he has promised in the deliverance of the people from bondage. The event will demonstrate that he is Lord of history. The name discloses who this God is. He is the Lord of history. Israel, too, has a name, and its meaning is probably "God rules" (Gen. 32:22-28). The historical God rules over the historical people, historical because he acts in this history of this people, and uses the realms of nature, where other peoples of the ancient Near East found the center of meaning for their lives, only as instruments for the realization of his historical purpose. It is not the cosmos with the repetitiveness of its rhythms, but history with the givenness of divinely intended events that is the sphere of Israel's faith and activity and expectation.

Yahweh's power and providence span the whole field of man's history, whether we think of individuals like Abraham, Moses, David, and Jeremiah, or of the people of Israel, or of the nations of the world. Every area is brought into subjection to his historical revelation and purpose. We see this very clearly in the way that originally secular laws have been placed in the context of Exodus and covenant or in the way in which ancient Oriental Wisdom is brought under the regnancy of Yahweh (Prov. 16:11; 17:3; 19:17; 24:17-18). We see it, too, in the way that ancient myths are historicized. Thus, the best known of all ancient Near Eastern myths, the myth of the chaos-dragon, is no longer understood as the primeval conflict between the deified forces of nature, but as Yahweh's victory over Egypt in his delivering his people from slavery. In a radical sense myth is transformed in the Old Testament as magic is transformed by the intervention of the personal will of a historical God.

Again, Yahweh wages battle against all the forces which seek to assert their independence over against him, whether they be the evil propensities of the heart of man, or the nations' claim to sovereignty, or the pride and power of the earthly kings. The world of demons is relegated to a position of only minor importance, and in contrast to other Near Eastern religions, man is delivered from the fear and dread of its destructive power. Finally, we witness the power of the Lord of history in the Old Testament by the absence of those modern disciplines which seek to comprehend the meaning of man's life or of his society by some rationale or intellectual structure. Properly speaking, the Bible contains no psychology or sociology or anthropology or political economy. When we use such terms in connection with the thought of ancient Israel, we speak as spectators viewing what we read from the outside. In reality we derive them from narrative and poetic materials in which the interest and way of thinking are quite different from those of modern scientific disciplines. Dominating the whole Old Testament with all its rich diversity is the persistence of a personal transcendent purpose.

The uniqueness and impressiveness of Israel's faith in Yahweh, the God of history, is further shown in the scope of the literary materials. As they lie before us today we have a chronological account from the creation of the world to the fall of the nation in 587 B.C., and beyond that to the point which Arnold J. Toynbee calls "the end of the Syriac time of troubles," that is, to the emergence of Cyrus II, the Persian king. Yet closer inspection of this long narrative reveals a vast variety of literary materials, emanating from many different sources, different temporal loci, different writers, and different proveniences. Late materials lie side by side with early, and, what is more, the sources are controlled by differing points of view and theologies. But, having done justice to the heterogeneity of the sources and literary forms, we must then go further and seek to comprehend the work as a whole. Having performed our task as critical historians, we must seek to gain a synoptic view of Israel's recorded history and to discern the creative forces which went to its final ordering and completion. We shall then see that the faith that persists throughout all the "historical" records is that God controls and disposes over history, orders and rules it in his ways, and calls man to responsibility in it. We shall see that history is the Word of God actualizing itself in events. That this faith is affirmed in the manner in which the Old Testament affirms it, in manifold forms and in many diverse situations, in the living language of narrative of various kinds and in the rich imagery of poetic speech, by men of different moods and tempers and social status, accounts, on one level at least, for its enduring fascination and vitality.

Not only the so-called historical books but also much of the rest of the Old Testament exhibits the same concern with history. Thus it is a basic principle of all modern interpretation that the prophets of Israel are to be understood against the background of their own times and in the light of the events of their own age. Failure to understand the prophets in this way makes them not only uninteresting and unintelligible, but also corrupts their intention and meaning. Such books as Isaiah and Jeremiah, for example, cannot be really understood without a knowledge of the events in Palestine and in the wider ranges of the ancient Near East. The poets of Israel also refer again and again to the central events of Israel's past, not because of their nostalgia for tradition or for aesthetic recollection, but because these events belong to the fabric of their consciousness as members of the historical people.

Historiography is not a scientific pursuit in Israel. Its purpose is not to identify the laws and principles which determine the course of events. It is not an analysis of society or a sociological study of its phenomenology. From the point of view of the modern secular historian, it is often poor history; perhaps this accounts for its frequent neglect by historians of the ancient world. It is astonishing to the historian to observe how important events are often either ignored or minimized and how apparently inconsequential and trivial events are magnified. At the end of the day it is often the word of some prophet which proves to be more powerful and effectual than the decrees and dictates of the mighty. Israel's historiography is of many kinds, but each kind has been placed within the framework of a controlling purpose. It is governed by man's responsibility in his present to his past and to his future, the time when he confronts an ultimate judgment upon his life and history.

Such a history as we have sought to describe demands response from Israel. She cannot escape it by fleeing into some realm of ideality, into the world of mysticism or the inner light, or by servitude to the past. *She must remember.* Without remembering there would be no history and therefore no revelation. What is remembered is not merely the annals and chronicles (of these there are relatively few in the Old Testament), but the saving *magnalia* and the meaning given to

them by the Word of God, either through the prophet or
through the priest. They are the ground of her existence and
the motivating power of her consciousness as a people. To put
it in another way, Israel thinks historically, but her thinking
is a remembering of the prior acts of God and an expecting
of what he yet will do.

Exodus, Election, and the Way of Israel

> Sing to Yahweh,
>   for he has triumphed mightily;
> the horse and its rider
>   he has cast into the sea.
>
> Exodus 15:21

> I am Yahweh your God, who brought you out of the land
> of Egypt.
>
> Exodus 20:2

> You yourselves have seen what I did to the Egyptians, how
> I bore you on wings of eagles, and brought you to me.
>
> Exodus 19:4

> Has any god ever attempted to go and take a nation for
> himself from the midst of another nation, by trials, by signs,
> by wonders, and by war, by a mighty hand and outstretched
> arm, and by great terrors, according to all that the Lord your
> God did for you in Egypt before your eyes?
>
> Deuteronomy 4:34

The Exodus of Israel from the land of Egypt is a meeting
and a revelation. A God performs a mighty deed for those who
are not yet a people. But more than that, he witnesses to his
deed. That is what he is doing on the occasion of the Bush,
and Miriam can sing so exultantly, not because she had made
a great discovery, but because Yahweh's Word to Moses is confirmed by his Deed. The Exodus was no deduction on the
part of a clever and gifted people from what had happened; it
was not Israel's interpretation of the meaning or significance
of what had occurred at the Sea of Reeds. What is recorded
of Israel's intellectual or moral insight does not, indeed, inspire

great confidence. The deed was revelation, and the meaning of the deed was revelation, which Israel appropriates by faith. The Invisible One had wrought his deed in time. Israel does not "dimly guess what Time in mists confounds," but listens to the sound of the trumpet "from the hid battlements of eternity." *Yahweh has done it!* That is her joyous cry of faith. *He has triumphed in mighty victory!* That is the song they sang antiphonally at the place of the Reeds. It was destined to sound and sound again throughout the course of the succeeding centuries. At the fountain sources of Israel's life was an event, and that event was the redemption from Egyptian bondage. It gave Israel new words, a new way of speaking, and a history. The Exodus is for Israel what the death and resurrection of the Christ are for the new Israel, and the new Israel could do no other than employ the imagery and words of the redemption from bondage when it proclaimed redemption from a deeper and more terrible slavery.

If one is tempted to raise the legitimate and necessary question, What was it that happened at the Sea of Reeds? then there is the equivocal answer that the historian is forced to give because he really does not know. There is also the answer that faith gives: "Our God delivered us from bondage." But what was it in Yahweh that prompted him to this deed? Why this people and no other? On one level, this is a mystery hidden in the heart and mind of God; on another, the answer is that God is initiating his purpose in man's history through this people. He is acting for his own purpose. But behind his purpose was his love for the people; it was love that moved him to act so. This is stated repeatedly in relatively late sources (Deut. 4:37; 7:6-11; 10:14-15), but it is implicit in earlier accounts. It is clear in his words to Moses at the Bush where he is at pains to recount the afflictions and distresses of Israel. Moses is not deeply moved, but Yahweh keeps on reminding him of his people's sufferings. To these he cannot be, must not be, heedless. God acted then out of his love for the people, and it is the motivation of his love that brought Israel into being, a love that she did not in any sense deserve. All love has its own mystery and its own sovereignty; definitions and explanations do not exhaust it. But it is not only Israel as a communal solidarity who knows this; every man of Israel also knows that as a member of the community of God he is the recipient of this love. This is why God can speak with the personal, singular, second-person "thou."

The hour of the Exodus was the birth of a people, the people chosen and called to a destiny. Israel's consciousness of being a people was first awakened at the Exodus; the event was the *fons et origo* of her life. The phenomenon of Israel in the world is not to be explained ethnologically in terms of race or blood, or culturally in terms of intellectual genius or "spiritual" aptitude, or mythologically in terms of a divine hero or demigod as a progenitor, or geographically in terms of the strategic physical situation she came to occupy in the land of Palestine, or sociologically in terms of a peculiarly dynamic history during the first millennium b.c. No, her beginning belongs to a divine action in history. He who belongs to this people belongs to history because he belongs to a solidarity which confesses this God of the Exodus to be Lord and King. But we cannot allow the matter to rest here. The Exodus is also a summons. In the event, Israel's vocation is pronounced. It is this consciousness of a call which explains the sense of mission and reponsibility in the faith of Israel. It is the ultimate source, too, of the ever-recurring calls of those who are its truest representatives.

In the event of the Exodus, the God of history laid his claim upon his people. The deed was surely a deed of grace, *sola gratia,* but its nature was such as to evoke response. Otherwise it could not have been truly appropriated, truly participated in, truly grasped. Israel knows herself as the redeemed and liberated community, the people in behalf of whom this God has spoken his Word to her and has fulfilled it in his deed for her. It is striking that the deliverance should play so cardinal a role in the faith of ancient Israel. Yet it was this event, above all others, that made her a people. Since it was the intervention of the divine action in history, history could never be meaningless or events merely fortuitous. It was an event once for all, but it was appropriated in the present; indeed it was the activating of the event into the present that rescued it from antiquarianism and sterility. But more than that, it pointed to Israel's destiny. It was a summons to Israel to become God's people and to fulfill the obligation of that summons. It was a call to allegiance, a call to service, a call to freedom, to the kind of service in which alone she could find freedom. The celebration of the commemoration of the event still resounds with the contemporaneity of the original event at the place of the Reeds.[1]

> In every generation one must look upon himself as if he personally had come forth from Egypt, in keeping with the biblical command, "And thou shalt tell thy son in that day, saying, it is because of that which the Lord did to *me* when I went forth from Egypt." For it was not alone our fathers whom the Holy One, blessed be He, redeemed, but also us whom He redeemed with them, as it is said, "And *us* He brought out thence that He might lead *us* to, and give *us*, the land which He swore to our fathers."

In numerous historical contexts, it is the liberation from slavery that guides and directs the movement of events (Josh. 2:10 ff.; 24; Judg. 6:11 ff.; I Sam. 4:5 ff.; 12; II Sam. 7:4 ff.; I Kings 6:1; 8; II Kings 17:35 ff.; Neh. 9:9 ff.). The little credo preserved in Deuteronomy 26:5-9 may well be the statement of faith that lies behind and determines the composition and structure of the Yahwist epic and the whole Hexateuch. In it, the Exodus is the central event. Other credos keep repeating the crucial words: Yahweh brought us out of Egypt. (Josh. 24; I Sam. 12; Ps. 105; Neh. 8 and others). They come to us characteristically in the forms of rituals and liturgies in which the community is called to participation and celebration. The same theme is echoed and re-echoed in many literary and historical contexts: invectives, exhortations, hymns, laments, legal statutes and directions, and the divine self-asseverations.

It is clear from all this that the Exodus was the motivating and inspiring event in Israel's past, the event in God's time for man, and the earnest of the future before her. But more than that, it was the inspiration of Israel's response. It is the free, gracious act of God that lies behind the covenant rituals (Exod. 19:3-8; 24:1-18), the Sinaitic Decalogue (Exod. 20:1-17; cf. Deut. 5:6-21), and indeed the vast corpus of legal material contained in the Pentateuch. Already in the Covenant Code, the apodictic law is motivated by memory of Egypt:

[1] *The Haggadah of the Passover,* edited by David and Tamar de Sola Pool, Bloch Publishing Company (New York, 1953), p. 51.

> You shall not wrong a stranger or oppress him, for you
> were strangers in the land of Egypt.
>
> Exodus 22:21;
Deuteronomy 10:18-19; Leviticus 19:33-34

The relatively merciful treatment of the liberated slave is in-
spired by the memory of Israel's slavery:

> You shall remember that you were a slave in the land of
> Egypt, and the Lord your God redeemed you: therefore I
> command you today.
>
> Deuteronomy 15:15

The same theme is repeated over and over again (Deut. 4:37 ff.;
5:14-15; 10:18-19). It is eloquently expressed in Deuteronomy:

> For you are a people holy to the Lord your God; the Lord
> your God has chosen you to be a people for his own posses-
> sion out of all the peoples that are on the face of the earth.
> It was not because you were more in number than any other
> people that the Lord set his love upon you and chose you,
> for you were the fewest of all peoples; but it is because God
> loves you, and is keeping the oath which he swore to your
> fathers, that the Lord has brought you out with a mighty
> hand, and redeemed you from the house of bondage, from
> the hand of Pharaoh king of Egypt. Know therefore that the
> Lord your God is God, the faithful God who keeps covenant
> and steadfast love with those who love him and keep his
> commandments to a thousand generations. . . . You shall
> therefore be careful to do the commandment, and the stat-
> utes, and the ordinances, which I command you this day.
>
> cf. Deuteronomy 7:6-11; 4:37 ff.; 11:1 ff

The love of God is to evoke Israel's answering love to him, and
this love expresses itself in the humanitarian legislation, which
is not mere legalism but the joyous response of obedience to
the love and compassion of God. To forget the demand for
obedience is to forget what God has done and to be heedless of
the love that motivated it (Deut. 8:11-20).

The prophets of Israel appeal to the great divine event at
the beginning of Israel's life as the motivation for their calls
to obedience and faithful allegiance. The Lord to whom and
for whom they bear their witness, who addresses Israel with
his will in every new situation, is the one who wrought mightily
in Egypt in Israel's behalf:

I am Yahweh your God
　　from the land of Egypt;
　　you know no God but me,
　　　　and besides me there is no savior.
Hosea 13:4; cf. 12:9

Israel's disobedience is gross ingratitude for what Yahweh has
done (Amos 2:10 ff.) . Jeremiah castigates the fathers of Israel
because they have deserted their God:

They did not say, "Where is Yahweh
　　who brought us out of the land of Egypt?"
Jeremiah 2:6; cf. Amos 2:10; 9:7;
Hosea 11:1 ff.; Micah 6:3-4;
Jeremiah 32:20-21; Ezekiel 20:3-8

　The election of Israel is deepened by its extension into the
earlier traditions and is heightened by its extension into the
future. So Abraham, the father, receives the promise fulfilled
in the Exodus; in him Israel already exists, and it is he who
walks where he is led, to the land promised to Israel. He is
the true Israel, and the election and the Exodus already belong
to him. And what is to be the denouement of Israel's election
life, the realization of the purpose declared in the Exodus,
but the new Exodus, when the ransomed of the Lord shall return to Zion, now the mountain of God (Sinai) , with singing
and great gladness? The prophet of the Exile sees the new age
inaugurated by the new Exodus:

Thus says the Lord,
　　who makes a way in the sea,
　　a path in the mighty waters,
who brings forth chariot and horse,
　　army and warrior; . . .

Remember not the former things,
　　nor consider the things of old.
Behold, I am doing a new thing;
　　now it springs forth, do you perceive it?
I will make a way in the wilderness
　　and rivers in the desert.
Isaiah 43:16-19

Again, the Exodus is the source of comfort and consolation to those who mourn and lament (Ps. 77:11-19; Isa. 63:11-14), as it is the chief inspiration to thanksgiving and joy (Pss. 66; 105; 106; 136; etc.). Israel lives in her obedience out of gratitude to her God for all the mighty works, but among these it is the redemption from bondage that occupies a position of pre-eminence.

In the annual celebration of the Passover, Israel experiences again the victory of her God at the Sea, and it becomes a living, contemporaneous event. The *magnalia Dei* are recounted in the Haggada of the fathers, they are dramatically repeated, and the joyous hymns are sung as once Miriam sang her *Jubilate Deo* when the Lord God of Israel had shown himself to be the Lord of history and had determined the direction in which Israel's life in the world was to move. In her participation and involvement, Israel took to herself the burdens that election required of her.

Covenant and People

Now therefore, if you will obey my voice and keep my covenant, you shall be my own possession among all peoples; for all the earth is mine, and you shall be to me a kingdom of priests and a holy nation.
Exodus 19:5-6a

Not with our fathers did Yahweh make this covenant, but with us, who are all of us here alive this day.
Deuteronomy 5:3

You shall be my people, and I will be your God.
Exodus 6:7, and *passim*

The deliverance from Egyptian bondage so dominates the many contexts we have been examining that it would seem to exhaust all other possibilities. Yet, in the present form of the traditions nothing is more apparent than that it serves only as prologue to all that is to follow at Sinai. Upon this all our sources agree. Sinai is the goal of the wandering from Egypt. In pillar of cloud by day and in pillar of fire by night, the Leader goes on before to lead his people to their destination. There the issue will be drawn, the choice offered, the decision made; there the words will be spoken, the answer required, and from there Israel will journey on to the land promised to her.

We cannot be certain of the etymology of the Hebrew word for covenant, *berith*. It may be derived from a verb meaning "to eat"; this would suit many early contexts very well. But we gain a clearer notion of what the covenant was from the many contexts in which covenants are mentioned, above all the narrative of Israel's entrance into covenant relationship with Yahweh at Sinai. We have been aided in recent years by the study of other ancient Near Eastern compacts, notably the Hittite treaties. (The Hebrew word for treaty and covenant is the same.) The king makes a treaty with his vassals after the model of the suzerainty compact. The general structure of the Hittite treaties is not dissimilar to the structure of the Exodus narrative.[2]

An early tradition reports the event as follows:

Thus shall you say to the house of Jacob,
    and speak to the sons of Israel:
You have seen for yourselves what I did to the Egyptians,
    how I bore you on eagles' wings,
    and brought you to me.
And now, if you will really listen to my voice,
    and keep my covenant
then you will become my own possession among all peoples,
    for all the earth is mine.
You shall become to me a kingdom of priests and a holy nation.

    These are the words you shall speak to the sons of Israel.
                                Exodus 19:3b-6

Yahweh appears in a great theophany, amidst thunders and lightnings and the sound of the trumpet. Moses speaks and God answers in the words of the Decalogue (Exod. 20:1-17). The laws of the Covenant Code follow (Exod. 20:23-23:33), and the covenant is concluded (Exod. 24:1-11). The intricate, composite account (Exod. 19-24) is by no means clear throughout,

---

[2] George E. Mendenhall, *Law and Covenant in Israel and the Ancient Near East.* The Biblical Colloquium (Pittsburgh, 1955), pp. 24-50.

but one cannot, in the midst of all the transcendent mystery, fail to sense the awesomeness and reality of the momentous event: *Yahweh becomes the God of Israel and Israel becomes the people of Yahweh.*

We may sketch the significance of the event in broad strokes.

1. Yahweh comes to Israel as King. He is seated as King on the throne of the ark *invisibly.* The invisible King is enthroned as sovereign over Israel. No spatial imagery is therefore to be employed for representing him:

> Since you saw no form on the day that the Lord spoke to you at Horeb out of the midst of the fire, beware lest you act corruptly by making a graven image for yourselves in the form of any figure.
> Deuteronomy 4:15-16a; cf. Exodus 20:4-6

Israel's decision then is a decision concerning a sovereignty which resists all spatial representation. The mystery of the divine rule in history must not be coerced into the things men devise to make God present and available. The answer Israel gives is an affirmation of allegiance to Yahweh as King over her history. An early hymn reported to have been sung my Moses and the people concludes with the affirmation of Israel's faith:

> The Lord will reign for ever and ever.
> Exodus 15:18

The words are later than the Mosaic age, but they preserve an authentic memory. The consequences of such an affirmation were momentous for Israel's history and for the history of the world.

2. At Sinai, Israel entered into relationship with the Invisible King Enthroned, the One who had revealed his Name to her, the Holy One who speaks. Thus, she was rescued from the perils of an ultimate isolation. She was tempted again and again throughout the course of her history to construe the relationship in ways that would unite her prematurely and without qualification to her God, but such corruptions evoked the protests of the prophets. The words of relation keep sounding throughout the Old Testament: "I will be your God, and

you shall be my people." God is related here, not to the soil and the hidden mysteries of life, not to a race, not to a *homo religiosus*, but to a people. Hosea and some of the prophets who followed him employ the familiar ancient Near Eastern category of the divine marriage to describe the relationship, but what is unique in Israel's faith is that a God enters into relation with a people and that the relationship is consummated by a decision. Israel lives by the consciousness that she belongs to the historical invisible King who reigns. When she is faithful to her vows, she is not stranded on the shoals of time, but lives in a relationship to the ultimate Lord. She lives by her belongingness.

3. The event at Sinai required decision. Israel was called to choose or reject. She must decide for or against this particular God of the Exodus and history. It was not merely a choice between one God and another god; it was a decision for this particular God or the gods of nature which the other nations of the ancient Near East worshiped. Again, it was a choice between One God and many gods. Israel's faith was to be centered in *one* allegiance, *one* sovereign, *one* Lord of history; she was therefore delivered from the confusions and distractions of divided loyalties and from the fears which haunt the hearts of the devotees of the polytheisms. What was required of her depended upon the will and purpose of the One who revealed himself, who demanded *exclusive* loyalty and allegiance, and who made clear the alternatives of devotion to him or to the gods of the nations.

4. We cannot be certain of the composition of the clans who met at Sinai, which of the tribes were present and which were not, though the likelihood is that they were primarily the Joseph tribes of Ephraim and Manasseh. We can be reasonably sure that they represented a diversity of elements, "a mixed multitude," as they are sometimes called (Exod. 12:38; cf. Num. 11:4). Together they now unite in a common decision and a common allegiance to one Lord. At Shechem, all the twelve tribes unite in their single words of fealty and fidelity:

The Lord our God we will serve, and his voice we will obey.

Joshua 24:24; cf. vss. 15, 18, 21

The bond which unites Israel is a common belonging to one
God, the Lord of her past and of her future. Israel is one in its
commitment to one God.

5. The covenant words pointed to the future: "I will be
your God, and you shall be my people." Israel is granted a
great assurance, and her existence is therefore one of confidence in the Lord who has assured her of his presence with
her. She can rely upon him because he is faithful and worthy
of trust; he is the Upholder and Sustainer of the covenant.

6. Israel's commitment to the covenant was voluntary and
free; nothing was said of any evil consequences that would follow if she rejected the relationship proffered her. In commit-
ting herself to a personal Lord who is at once transcendent to
history yet active within it, to One who is sovereign over history and powerful to achieve his purpose, Israel was free from
an ultimate fear or ultimate bondage to any temporal power.
She was free in covenantal bondage; slavery to Pharaoh was
slavery indeed, slavery to God was an infinitely different matter.
In acknowledging his Lordship and rule, she could always resort to a higher court of appeal; she could view the economic,
social, political, and international order from the standpoint
of the Lord of history; she could live by the knowledge that his
will was decisive for her and that it was his purpose that was
central to her understanding of her existence. This meant that
her national life existed under radical tensions with the faith
of the covenant, for the temporal order constantly contradicted
that faith. Yet her life in covenant was completely oriented
to God's sovereignty and grace.

Throughout the course of Israel's history the covenant serves
as a source of transcendent criticism over the whole of life. The
relativities of history could never assume an absolute status
without the trenchant criticism of those who had been called
by the covenant Lord to speak his word to the situation. The
more confusing and perplexing the political situation, the
deeper the national crisis, and the nearer the abyss of destruction, the more clearly and passionately did the prophets of
Israel proclaim the primacy and pertinence of the covenant.
Kings, judges, priests, prophets; trade and commerce; domestic
affairs and foreign policy; institutions, even the most venerated
and sacred—all came under the attack of the prophet sent of

God. This was possible only because of the prior allegiance to an ultimate source of justice, the personal Subject to whom Israel had once replied:

> All that the Lord has spoken we will do.
>
> Exodus 19:8

7. The ethical terminology of the Old Testament is derived in large part from the covenant relationship. In almost every instance it is a terminology signifying a relationship between God and his people. Primary among these words is *hesed*, which is susceptible of many renderings, often depending upon the context in which it is used. It can mean kindness, covenant love, steadfast love, devotion, fidelity, even grace. It bears the connotation of stability, strength, and firmness, and is associated not infrequently with truth (*' emeth*), which also bears this connotation. It is the strength which gives stability to the relationship, and it is therefore the gift of God to his people. To God's *hesed* they appeal who desire him to confirm the relation; they can appeal to Yahweh for his *hesed* because it has been manifested in the covenant bond. *Hesed* is God's gift to Israel, and Israel answers his *hesed* by turning to him in loyalty, repentance, and obedience.

Associated with *hesed* is faithfulness (*' emunah*). Faithfulness means fulfilling the obligations of covenant allegiance. He is faithful who maintains the covenant, upholds it, and lives in conformity with the relationship of those who participate in it. It is Yahweh's faithfulness to his covenant that gives the Israelite confidence and trust and security. The righteous man lives by his faithfulness (Hab. 2:4b), that is, by his complete trust and confidence in him who is faithful. Faithfulness is participating actively in God's purpose and plan. After recounting all the affliction and despair he has endured, the rejection and bitterness which obsess him, the suppliant can appeal to God's covenant grace:

> The steadfast love of the Lord never ceases (RSV),
>   his mercies never come to an end;
> they are new every morning;
>   great is thy faithfulness.
>
> Lamentations 3:22

Righteousness (*ṣedaqah*), too, is a covenant word, though not, of course, exclusively so, and it, too, denotes a relation. To be righteous is to fulfill the demands of the relationship. Yahweh is righteous because he is faithful to his covenant and fulfills what is required in the relationship. Thus the righteous deeds of Yahweh are his saving acts, his victories, all that he does to create and establish and perpetuate community. He who obeys the Torah, the revealed law implementing the covenant, is righteous. Closely related to righteousness and often scarcely distinguishable from it is justice (*mishpaṭ*). It also has a wide range of meaning: custom, manner, way of acting, decision, judicial sentence, ordinance, right. It is the function of the judge (*shopheṭ*) to render a just decision (*mishpaṭ*), the right that is due every man as a member of the community of brothers. Every man has his own right; it belongs to him as a man in covenant with other men in the common bond with Yahweh. The foundations of the royal throne are righteousness and justice.

Another word with a variety of meanings but one intimately associated with the covenant is *shalom*, frequently translated by "peace," although its meaning is more extensive. It often means prosperity, completeness, tranquility, welfare, even friendship, but in covenantal contexts well-being. It is the covenant that secures and establishes *shalom*. It is this well-being that gives stability to the relationship, and as such it is the gift of God to his people. The later prophets look forward to a *berith shalom,* a covenant of well-being and peace. Yahweh promises peace and well-being to his people.

We need refer to one more term which characterizes the covenant in a special way: knowledge. This, too, is a word of relation, and never refers to intellectual, theoretical, or speculative knowing. To know God is to hear him and to respond to his prior knowledge. Knowledge of God (*da'ath 'elohim*) is an all-inclusive term tantamount to religion. He who truly knows God serves him, trusts him, does his will, walks in his way, and acknowledges him to be his Lord and King. Above all else is the knowledge which love creates. It is an interior knowing. To know God is to love him, to love his testimonies, to love him for his prior love and his demonstration of it in his acts. Hosea combines many of the great covenant words of Israel in his use of the marriage symbol. Here we see very clearly what it means to know God:

And I will betroth you to me for ever;
   and I will betroth you to me in righteousness and in justice,
   in steadfast love and in compassion.
And I will betroth you to me in faithfulness,
   and you shall know the Lord.

Hosea 2:19-20

Jeremiah tells of a king who exemplified the knowing of God:

    He judged the cause of the poor and needy;
      then it was well.
    Is not this to know me?
      says the Lord.

Jeremiah 22:16

The covenant was initiated as an act of divine grace. But it also provided the basis upon which Israel was summoned to live responsibly in history under the active rule of Yahweh. At the heart of the bond was the condition: "If you will truly obey my voice and keep my covenant, then you shall become my precious possession, a kingdom of priests, and a holy people" (Exod. 19:5). The covenant is contingent, contingent upon obedience and fidelity. It pointed to a future and a consummation, surely, but the future was to be determined by Israel's response to the divine demand as it was formulated in the teachings of the Torah. Nevertheless, Israel cannot abrogate the covenant, and because this is so, the way is open to transcending it by an act of grace.

As the Passover feast commemorated the Exodus from Egypt and made it a present and living reality in the lives of faithful Israelites, so the events associated with Sinai were remembered at the Feast of Tabernacles. Once in every seven years (Deut. 31:10-11; Lev. 23:43-44), Israel would gather to give heed to the reading of the law, to listen to the sound of the *shophar* (recalling the trumpet blast on the occasion of Yahweh's self-disclosure), and to participate in the ceremonies of the conclusion of the covenant. Thus the ancient events were again contemporary. History was proclaimed, re-lived, re-experienced; the events became alive in speaking; and in hearing the words spoken, Israel became united with those who once beheld and trembled, listened and were called to decision, entered into covenant, and thus were committed in solemn dedication to serve and obey their King and Judge and Liberator.

4
The Way of the Leaders

THE SENSE OF OBLIGATION LIES DEEP IN THE heart of every man, sometimes obscurely, sometimes distraughtly or oppressively, but, to some degree or another, however variously conceived or deeply felt, it belongs to the interior fabric of his consciousness. Whenever he is disposed to be reflective or thoughtful concerning himself, he is aware that he has done those things which he ought not to have done and has left undone those things which he ought to have done. "What ought I to do?" belongs to the native speech of man. Not Eve alone or Cain alone hears the voice, "What have you done?" All of us have listened to those words, and have been confused or embarrassed or stricken by them. What is it, then, that is required of us? Israel's way is to change our neutral and impersonal passives into the personal ultimate active: "What does the Lord require? What is his will and purpose for me?" To these questions the whole Old Testament, from first page to last, gives its urgent and impassioned reply. For turn where we will—to the earliest legends and traditions of the patriarchs; to the teachings of the leaders (whether parent, judge, king, or priest) ; to the narratives of the historians; to the calls, oracles, and visions of the prophets sent of God; to the hymns, prayers, and thanksgivings of the cultic ministrants; to the counsels and directions of the wise—everywhere we encounter, in one form or another, the categorical "thou shalt" and "thou shalt not." Everywhere Israel is summoned to hearing: "Hear, O Israel!" The imperative and the vocative belong together, for words are being spoken to which man must give heed, and they are words addressed to him.

THE WAY OF THE LAWGIVERS

Consider the way of the Torah. Until relatively recently the Christian community has neglected this portion of its Scriptures, and what is more, it has often misunderstood and misapprehended its meaning and significance. Yet the Old Testament contains much law, and its influence is felt in all parts of the Bible. The religious faith of Israel is incomprehensible without the law. That there were laws of many kinds, some of which have little or no meaning for modern man, is surely true, but it would be unjust to identify the law only with its more primitive and outgrown ordinances and regulations. Moreover, many even of these latter regulations have a meaning for the devout son of Israel which it is hard for those outside Israel to appreciate. Their observance is Israel's witness to its vocation and solidarity as a holy people.

The legal literature of ancient Israel emanates from different times, different cultural contexts, and, as we have seen, it appears in many styles and forms. It does not offer itself as a law for mankind. It does not find its origin in natural law or in the orders of creation, although there are more than adumbrations of such a view (cf. Jer. 31:35-37). What is more surprising is that it is not royal law. The kings are not its creators and promulgators. Rather, Old Testament law is divine law.

Among the other peoples of the ancient Near East the deity is also the giver of the law. So in the famous stele of Hammurabi we see Shamash, the sun god, presenting the collection of laws to the Babylonian king. As in Israel, the god maintains and upholds the law, and is particularly concerned for those who are most liable to lose their rights. It is the greatness of Mesopotamian law that the source of justice resides in the deity, not in man. Kittu and Mesharu are the deifications of law and justice. It is important, therefore, not to exaggerate the distinctiveness of Israel's law. The concern for justice and the sense of compassion and pity is certainly not absent from the other legal collections; on the contrary, the king knows that he is the shepherd of his people and is charged with the responsibility of securing their rights.

In the collections of Ur Nammu, Lipit Ishtar, Eshnunna, and Hammurabi, the king receives the laws from the gods, but it is he who promulgates it. Not so in Israel. Moses is the mediator of the covenant, and in that role receives the laws for Israel. It is not to Moses or to a king or to a legislative body that Israel is responsible, but to God. Covenant community preceded the nation or kingdom, and the kingship never exercised a decisive influence upon law. God has revealed his will in the law, and Israel is summoned to respond to it. Thus she can always appeal to the higher sovereignty to which rulers and judges must also bow.

God is a God of justice (Isa. 30:18). The whole of Israel's existence is placed under the regnancy and providence of his justice. The Lord of all the earth does justice (Gen. 18:25). He judges and rules in accordance with his covenant with Israel (Psa. 7:12; Jer. 12:1); he loves justice and hates iniquity (Isa. 61:8). It is an unrelinquishable affirmation of biblical faith—an affirmation that brings all parts of the Old Testament with its many streams of tradition into a unity—that it is he who determines the right, upholds and establishes it, and rules the world of history by it. He is Lord of the right, and active participant in the right.

> The Rock, his work is perfect,
>   for all his ways are justice.
> A trustworthy God without iniquity,
>   just and right is he.
>
>   Deuteronomy 32:4

God is not exalted in splendid isolation from his people; he condescends to man's history and man's estate, above all to the humble and contrite, to the needy and to those who have no friend in court (Isa. 57:15). To understand the meaning of Torah in the Bible, then, we must see it in the light of the living, personal, historical relationship between Yahweh and Israel. As the Holy One of Israel, he consecrates his people to obedience and service and separateness from the ways of the nations; as King, he rules the world with justice and the peoples with his truth; as Father, he exercises his power and authority, yet with compassion and love; as Leader on the Way, he guides his people on its way through history; as Teacher, he grasps the pupil by the hand and instructs him, and subjects him to his firm but merciful discipline. It is this God to whom Israel is urged to listen, the God who granted the inspiration and motivation to obedience in the glad good news of liberation from slavery and who provided the basis for allegiance and fidelity in the covenant at Sinai.

An examination of the laws of Israel and their interpretations makes it clear that the relationship is not merely legal.
Juristic categories do not exhaust the meaning of the bond.
We must often think, rather, of the relationship within the
family with its obligations and its bonds of compassion, understanding, and love. The God of Israel does not simply meet
his people with an unequivocal *do ut des*. On the contrary,
the commands are frequently expanded by subordinate clauses
of various forms supplying the motivations for the conduct
that is required. In the categorical manner of the apodictic
laws Israel is commanded: "Thou shalt take no bribe"; and
then come the words of explanation: "for a bribe blinds the
officials, and subverts the cause of those who are in the right"
(Exod. 23:8). Or take the command against beating a man
with more than forty stripes. This is sternly forbidden: "lest
if one should go on to beat him with more stripes than these,
your brother be degraded in your sight" (Deut. 25:3). There
is great stress on honesty in trade, especially on the full and
just weight and the full and just measure, in order that Israel
may live long in the land given to her. But then we are given
the reason for the prohibition of dishonesty: "For all who do
such things, all who act dishonestly, are an abomination to the
Lord your God" (Deut. 25:15-16). Or take this word of compassion: "No man shall take a mill or an upper-millstone in
pledge, for he would be taking a life in pledge" (Deut. 24:6).

There are other motivations or reasons for obedience. Chief
of these is the frequent appeal to the events of the age of
Moses, especially the liberation from slavery, but other events
of that period also. Thus the law on Sabbath observance and
the prohibition against labor in the Deuteronomic version of
the Decalogue are not only expanded with the merciful words
"that your manservant and maidservant may rest as well as
you," but also by the reference to the time of bondage: "You
shall remember that you were a servant in the land of Egypt,
and the Lord your God brought you out thence with a mighty
hand, and an outstretched arm; therefore the Lord your God
commanded you to keep the sabbath day" (Deut. 5:12-15).
More than thirty such motivations appear in the laws, so one
cannot resist the conclusion that the age of Moses was con-
sidered normative for Israel's future. Ethics is grounded his-

torically. The antiphon "I am Yahweh your God" which appears so frequently after the individual laws in the Holiness Code is an emphatic reminder to Israel that one will dominates the whole of its life. It is meant as a word of authority and sovereignty. Obedience springs from faith and allegiance, and Israel's response is one of gratitude and awe, devotion and thanksgiving.

Now it is striking that these motivations are completely absent from the other Near Eastern compilations. They are distinctively Israelite, as an examination of their contents confirms. Moreover, they are not designed for the direction of priest or judge or other official, but are addressed to the people. They are democratic in intent. Yahweh does indeed desire and ask obedience, but he also desires men who understand his ordinance, that is, "men who also confirm them inwardly."[1] One feels this throughout Deuteronomy. There God is constantly urging his people on to obedience and trust, but also encouraging them, reminding them, in season and out, of the love that brought them to birth, of their weakness and apostasy, but also of the strength by which they may be strong. He speaks of the nearness of his Word, a nearness which they came to know at Sinai, which was awe and dread indeed, but also a drawing near in communion because of the holy *pathos* within him to create a people in the world to be the means of his revealing to men:

> For this commandment which I command you this day is not too hard for you, neither is it far off. It is not in heaven, that you should say, "Who will go up for us to heaven, and bring it to us, that we may hear it and do it?" Neither is it beyond the sea, that you should say, "Who will go over the sea for us, and bring it to us, that we may hear and do it?" But the word is very near you; it is in your mouth and in your heart, *so that you can do it.*
>
> Deuteronomy 30:11-14

Such optimism as to man's ability to do what he ought to do is surely not typical of some other parts of the Bible. Prophets like Jeremiah and Ezekiel were far from being so confident.

[1] Gerhard von Rad, *Theologie des alten Testaments* (1957), I, pp. 199ff.; B. Gemser, "The Importance of the Motive Clause in Old Testament Law," Supplements to Vetus Testamentum, *Congress Volume* (Munich: Chr. Kaiser Verlag, 1953), pp. 50-66.

At the place of the meeting, Yahweh speaks to Israel. The Decalogue (Exod. 20:1-17) not only occupies the strategic position in the composite account of the covenant (Exod. 19-24) but is also the climax of the long narrative beginning with the call of Moses (Exod. 3-4). The words of the theophany which introduce it are freighted with awesome mystery. Only when they are deeply heard does one sense the decisive centrality of the Decalogue which follows. Yahweh's coming into man's history through his election of Israel is now consummated; that is the meaning of his opening words in the first person: "I am Yahweh your God who brought you out of the land of Egypt." God has a word to speak of himself, and it is such a word as only the Liberator could speak. Israel hears the Name. Thus a relation is established. But she also hears that she is the people delivered and redeemed from slavery. Only then do the commands follow, and in the categorical form of the apodictic laws. There is no sufficient reason for denying their authenticity; they are the foundation of Mosaic faith.[2] In the worship of the Temple, these words were proclaimed, and each time they were heard Israel stood again at the foot of the mount where once they were spoken.

In the Covenant Code (Exod. 21-23) the whole of life is brought under the rule of God. Many of the laws are cultic. Some have the stamp of primitiveness upon them, others rise to heights of ethical grandeur. With the exception of the provisions for the slave, there is no class legislation here. It might be contended that this is due to the nomadic heritage lying behind them, but it is significant that this feature persisted and was elaborated in the rest of the Old Testament. Rich or poor, small or great, all Israelites are equal before God. The laws apply equally to all members of the community (Exod. 21:23-25; cf. Deut. 19:21; Lev. 24:19-20). The liberation from bondage has produced its first effect upon Israel's communal life: *all men are equal under God.* But there is a second feature of this Code which is quite as striking and one which also runs its course through the Old Testament: the prevailing concern for the oppressed, the disinherited, the weak, the poor and

---

[2] See H. H. Rowley, "Moses and the Decalogue," *Bulletin of the John Rylands Library,* Vol. 34, No. 1 (Manchester: The Manchester University Press, 1951).

afflicted. It is notable that the words are in apodictic form, but more than that, the sound of compassion, already heard in Yahweh's call to Moses at the Bush, is heard again. The memory of Egypt is in the mind of God:

> You shall not wrong a stranger or oppress him, for you were strangers in the land of Egypt.
> > Exodus 22:21; 23:9

> You shall not afflict any widow or orphan. If you do afflict them, and they cry out to me, I will surely hear their cry.
> > Exodus 22:22-23

It is significant that the command about the alien is repeated. In the later Codes, both commands are repeated and expanded. The resident foreigner, the fatherless, and the widow rejoice before Yahweh in the celebrations of the festivals (cf., e.g., Deut. 16:9-15). The same compassion is heard elsewhere: from the poor neighbor no interest is to be exacted; if the neighbor's garment is taken from him in pledge it must be restored before nightfall

> for that is his only covering, it is his mantle for his body; in what else shall he sleep? And if he cries to me, I will hear, for I am compassionate [*ki ḥanun 'ani*].
> > Exodus 22:25-27

To what age we are to assign such words it is difficult to say, but there is good reason to believe that they come from before the monarchy, possibly from the time of the occupation of the land or earlier.

It must be admitted that there are teachings of quite another mood and accent, but we cannot doubt that already in a very early period the divine compassion demonstrated in the liberation of the slaves exercised a formative influence upon Israel's moral consciousness. It was much more than a release from the grueling labor under the whip of the Egyptian taskmaster. It was release to freedom, interior release, a release with ethical consequences. Persons have their own inalienable dignity because God is concerned about them and goes out of his way to see that their rights are upheld, that they are cared for and treated justly, and that they are not discriminated against. Walter Eichrodt has stated the significance of the early laws succinctly:

> The human being, called by God to freedom, is the indispensable form of wealth—this is the kernel of the whole legal ideology of the Old Testament. The equality of all members of the nation before God who is no respector of persons, demands the same rights in working life; it calls for voluntary sacrifice of all citizens, in order to avert the inroads of inequality and oppression.[3]

But there is more. Even the enemy must be treated as a neighbor, and the faithful Israelite is under obligation to render him the justice that is his due, to treat him as a brother within the brotherhood of the called and consecrated people (Exod. 23:4-5). This is the justice of God.

The Deuteronomic Code is, in part at least, a homiletical expansion and re-interpretation of the Covenant Code. It has been generally identified with the Book of the Law discovered by Hilkiah the priest in the year 621 B.C., but its nucleus is probably earlier, possibly as early as the eighth century B.C. It is held by some scholars that it was taken to Jerusalem by the fugitives after the fall of Samaria in the year 722 B.C. Be that as it may, Deuteronomy has as its avowed intent a restoration of the faith of the Mosaic age. Here, as in the Covenant Code, we find cultic and moral laws, primitive and ethically advanced ordinances, side by side. The motivation for obedience, as we have had occasion to observe, is the love of God for his people. Israel is called to respond to Yahweh's prior love by loving him. It is clear that this involves the love of the brother. Yahweh is a holy God, but his holiness manifests itself not only in the *magnalia* of the election-covenant past but also in the righteousness and justice which were the way of his relating himself to his people.

The justice of God is to evoke Israel's justice. The fulfillment of the laws is by no means an external matter of mere conformity to what is required; rather, it must be an expression of the sincerity of the heart, the seat of will and thought. So the commands are the divine "testing" of Israel's fidelity and devotion:

[3] Walter Eichrodt, *What is the Social Message of the Old Testament?* (Geneva: World Council of Churches, 1949), p. 4.

> And you shall remember all the way which the Lord your God has led you these forty years in the wilderness, that he might humble you, testing you to know *what was in your heart,* whether you would keep his commandments or not.
>
> Deuteronomy 8:3

Nowhere is the demand for justice more impassioned and stirring than in Deuteronomy:

> Justice, only justice you must pursue in order that you may live and may possess the land which the Lord your God is giving you.
>
> Deuteronomy 16:20

The occupation of the land is constantly associated with the ethical responsibility of those to whom it has been promised, albeit contingently. The divine conditions are repeated often and in many different contexts, not in a legalistic manner, but as a constant call to present memory of the nature of the relation between Yahweh and people:

> And if you will obey my commandments which I command you this day, to love the Lord your God, and to serve him with all your heart and with all your soul, he will give you the rain for your land in its season, the early rain and the later rain, that you may gather in your grain and your wine and your oil.
>
> Deuteronomy 11:13f; cf. Deuteronomy 8:11-20;
> 11:22-25, 26-28; 28:1-6, 15-19, 58-60; 30:15-20

Here, as often elsewhere in the Old Testament, the life-giving forces within the soil are related to the conduct of those who possess it (cf. Amos 4:6-12; Hos. 2:6 ff., 17 ff.). The fertilizing rains are the divine gift to the faithful and obedient.

There must be no partiality in the administration of justice. This is stressed in the earliest legal formulations and continues its course not only in the rest of the laws but also in the prophets and wise men of Israel. Since God shows no partiality, so Israel must not "recognize faces," but must act impartially, without regard to rich or poor, patrician or peasant, great or small:

> Hear the cases between your brothers, and judge right-eously between a man and his brother or the alien that is

with him. You shall not be partial in judgment; you shall
hear the small and the great alike; you shall not be afraid
of the face of a man, for the judgment belongs to God; and
the case that is too hard for you, you shall bring to me, and
I will hear it.

Deuteronomy 1:16-18; cf. 16:19 and Ps. 82:2

The movement of these lines is noteworthy: first the repeated
imperatives, then the apodictic commands, both positive and
negative, then the statement of the basis for all justice, "for
judgment belongs to God," and finally the consideration of
cases that are too difficult for men to decide. Such words are
characteristic of the biblical way of speaking.

Nothing is more clear than that the God of Israel has a
special concern for the weak, the poor, the disinherited, the
alien, and all who stand in need. He is concerned for the welfare and well-being of all. Special provision must be made for
the landless, the widow, the orphan, and for all who have no
power in themselves to press their claims. We seem to be hearing again the echoes of the divine solicitude for Israel in the
time of her suffering and grief (Exod. 3:7-10). Deuteronomy
expands the old command in the Covenant Code about the
slave. When the time comes that he is to be liberated,

you shall not let him go empty-handed; you shall furnish
him liberally out of your flock, out of your threshing-floor,
and out of your wine press; as the Lord your God has blessed
you, you shall give to him. You shall remember that you
were a slave in the land of Egypt, and the Lord has redeemed
you; therefore I command you this day.

Deuteronomy 15:12-15

Every seven years all debts are to be remitted! One must not
refuse a loan to his poor neighbor because the year of release
is approaching. That would be a base thought. "You must give
to him freely, and you must not be grudging when you give"
(Deut. 15:1-11). Injustices within the family are candidly exposed, particularly in matters of inheritance (Deut. 21:15-17).
The case of the rebellious and insubordinate son is dealt with
very harshly (Deut. 21:18-21). On the other hand, even animals and birds come under the divine providence (Deut. 22:4,
6-7; 25:4). Sexual crimes are also exposed, and cultic prosti-

tution is rigorously forbidden (Deut. 23:17-18). They are an abomination to God, and they must be an abomination to Israel also.

Yahweh's justice and love are applied to numerous situations. What makes Deuteronomy so impressive is that it never fails to enumerate specifically and in detail how the divine justice and love apply to the exigencies of daily human existence. The keeping of the Torah is the way to life. Man lives by every word coming from the mouth of God, and it is very clear that this refers in the main to obedience and service, to what God has commanded in his teaching (Deut. 8:3). To be sure, life often refers to prosperity and success—the Old Testament is realistic in such matters—but elsewhere it means much more. Yahweh's words must be taken to heart. The law is nothing with which man may trifle. *It is your life* (Deut. 32:45-47). The choice between obedience and disobedience is fateful:

> See, I have set before you this day life and good, death and evil. . . . *Therefore choose life.*
> Deuteronomy 30:15, 19

The law is not only the source of life and the way to life. It is also the source of Israel's thanksgiving and joy. Indeed, the primary motive for obedience and service is Israel's gratitude for the unmerited gift of the acts of God and for the light of revelation he has granted in making his will and purpose known. Israel rejoices in the goodness of God because she discerns that all his revelation in deed and in word is a demonstration of the love that he bears her, and that this love is the power that rules over her life and history. It is true that Deuteronomy had its shortcomings and even more true that it was subject to deep corruption and abuse, but all in all it is an authentic expression of Hebraism, gathering as it does the memories of the sacred past and making them forever new and present to all who listen to its eloquent proclamations, and pointing as it does to a future in which Yahweh will send covenant mediators like Moses to proclaim anew what it is that is required of his people.

Israel did not permit the revelation to remain confined to an hour in human history, but in the celebrations of the Taber-

nacles listens again to what was once spoken to her at Horeb
(Deut. 31:9-13). The covenant with all its requirements was
renewed each time the community gathered in celebration.
History as the realm of the divine revealing was directed on
its course by a guiding hand, and in the midst of its confusing
and baffling events a Voice called out from beyond, urging
man to choose life:

> loving the Lord your God, obeying his voice, and cleaving
> to him; for that means life to you and length of days, that
> you may dwell in the land which the Lord swore to your
> fathers, to Abraham, to Isaac, and to Jacob, to give them.
>   Deuteronomy 30:20

The Way of the Prophets

The purpose of the divine activity in human history was
initiated in the *magnalia:* in the event of liberation God performed a deed which started Israel on its way through history
by demonstrating that he was history's Lord, and to it Israel
responded in a confessional of singing; in the covenanting at
Sinai he entered into a relationship with a people and thus
made it the historical people par excellence, and Israel responded with her decision of commitment; in the gracious gift
of the Torah, God granted Israel the guidance, direction, and
providential care she needed if she were to live by his Word,
fulfill the demands of the commission, and walk the road of
destiny appointed for her, and Israel responded by her awareness that she was responsible to a transcendent Sovereign. But
the divine Leader did not thereupon leave history to itself,
unattended and self-sufficient. In the worship of the sanctuary,
he was present. There the people answered in words and deeds
the Word and Deed of Yahweh. Yahweh was present to help,
to redeem, to forgive, and to speak his Word in the immediacy
of the hour.

But Yahweh did yet more for his people in ever-recurring
events and crises: he sent them his servants the prophets. The
prophets were appointed as his representatives to bear witness
to the mighty deeds of the past; they came with a particular
word for a particular time. In those hours when history stood
at the edge of the abyss or entered into the darkness or came

to the end of the road, they saw the Holy One enthroned in majesty and power over history (I Kings 22:19; Isa. 6:1-8). They did not come with a program of social reconstruction, an expert design for a new social order, with a political constitution for a democratic society, or with an economic system applicable to all situations.

The prophets came rather to proclaim the divine Lordship over time and event, to point to God's future and the establishment of his righteous rule in the earth, to call Israel to the place of decision, to pronounce divine judgment upon her rebellion and unfaithfulness, and to remind her of the destiny to which she had been called. They summoned Israel to remember the living sources of its life and to live in expectation of the fulfillment and resolution of the divine righteous will among men. They were messengers sent with a message from the Invisible One Enthroned. They were sent to speak for the Speaking One, whose Word would accomplish its purpose. Like Israel, they were chosen for service, called to responsibility, consecrated to be set apart from the people yet always intimately involved in their lives, appointed, too, as representatives of the people in their intercessions, and fated to bear the heavy burden of being chosen. They bear within them the storm and stress of perilous times, and walk the road of suffering, rejection, and isolation:

> For to all to whom I send you, you shall go,
>   and whatever I command you, you shall speak.
> Behold, I have put my words in your mouth.
> See, I have set you this day over nations and over kingdoms,
>   to pluck up and to break down,
>   to destroy and to overthrow,
>   to build and to plant.
>
> Jeremiah 1:7b, 9b-10

The ethical foundations of the prophetic proclamation may be stated in another way. One God, and only one God, is Lord over history, and wills to make himself known in history. This one God manifests his holiness in justice and righteousness, but is also compassionate and faithful. The love that demonstrated its power in the past still guides and directs the course of Israel's history. *Prophetic faith is faith in a singular, transcendent, holy, absolutely righteous God,* a God who wills to live in community and to create his community among men. It is a response to One who inspires faith and trust and confidence. That responsibility should be so centered in a transcendent power whose will was the ultimate norm for human conduct, and that this will should be directed to the events of history, were of vast importance for ethical development. No other people had anything which remotely approached Israel in the profundity and vitality of the ethical foundations of its life.

What, then, do the prophets have to say about God's will and intention? To such a question there are many answers. Israel ought to do good and hate evil (Amos 5:14-15); it ought to choose right and reject wrong (Amos 3:10; Mic. 3:9 ff.). There are those who hate the good and love the evil, who reverse the divine order by calling evil good and good evil, who put darkness for light and light for darkness, and thus set at nought the divine imperatives (Isa. 5:20-23). But the prophets refuse to be content with such formulations; they would never have been willing to abstract such statements from their contexts. They will not have their message reduced to platitudes or moral generalizations. Indeed, it is precarious to seize upon such statements and to allow them to determine what the prophets have to say, for men have an inveterate propensity to cavil over what is good and what is evil. Isaiah is right: they will call evil good and good evil.

Prophetic ethics is most itself when it is most concrete, indeed when it is most offensive to those who appeal to generalizations to be good. When Amos cries out, "Seek good and not evil that you may live," the context makes it clear precisely what he means. It means establishing justice *in the gate,* where the poor were being deprived of their rights (cf. Exod. 22:20-26; 23:6-9; Deut. 24:14-15, 17-22). It means "to seek the Lord and live," to bring into effect and to implement the basic rights which belong to every man in the community. The prophets keep calling for justice, justice for every man, and especially for those most liable to be treated unjustly, but they spell out what justice means in the particular situation, and they can do so with such passion and wrath because they speak

for the God of justice and compassion who intervenes in behalf of the exploited and weak and defenseless. They speak to
the time to which God has sent them, and their words are directed to the conditions of that time. Thus Elijah has a word
to speak to his age and Hosea to his, and their words are rela-
tive to, and relevant for, those times. A historical revelation
means to be concrete and relevant to particular history.

What is it, then, that Israel ought to do? The prophets would
answer that she *ought* to walk the good road that leads to
Sinai; she *ought* to live out of gratitude for what is vouchsafed
her; she *ought* to keep covenant and to obey the injunctions
of the Teaching; she *ought* to live as God wills her to live, in
conformity to his righteous purpose; she *ought* to continue to
give allegiance to the One to whom she has committed her life
and destiny. What makes the message of the prophets so com-
pelling is not only that they speak with passion and earnestness,
but also that they direct their attention to every facet of Israel's
historical life. Nothing is exempt from their piercing scrutiny.
If we seek to express the prophetic indictment against their
contemporaries, we may formulate it in a word: *they have
broken the covenant and transgressed the Torah* (I Kings
19:10, 14; Hos. 8:1; Jer. 31:32). To these words all the rest
are commentary.

We shall confine our attention to five of the areas to which
the prophets of Israel address themselves in the name of the
God who has called them to be his messengers. They offer no
social or cultural diagnoses, no psychological analyses of the
mind and heart of man, though their insight into human mo-
tives and ambitions is acute. It is extraordinary how this God
of Israel speaks the language of history. He knows the events
of the ancient Near Eastern world as well as the events within
Israel and Judah, he mentions the names of king and com-
moner alike. And always he speaks *in medias res.*

1. *The political order.* In the period of the settlement the
memories of the past were preserved in the amphictyony of
the twelve tribes at the central sanctuary of Shechem. There
the victorious deeds of Yahweh were celebrated, the Teaching
proclaimed, and the first fruits of the ground offered in grateful recognition of Yahweh's gift of the land. However, the
amphictyony was but a loose federation; only in times of crisis

did the tribes unite in Holy War. When the political situation grew precarious with the invasion of other peoples, notably the Philistines, the loose structure failed to meet the threat to Israel's existence. It was not unnatural, therefore, that the demand should be made for a new order of life. So the men of Israel approached Gideon and asked him to be their king, but he replied in the authentic speech of a son of the covenant: "I will not rule over you, and my son will not rule over you, Yahweh will reign over you" (Judg. 8:22-23) . Yahweh is King in Israel! Later the tribes made the same request of Samuel. In distress he prayed to Yahweh and received the answer: "Hearken to the voice of the people in all that they say to you; for they have not rejected you, but they have rejected me from being king over them" (I Sam. 8:7) .

The kingdom was a threat to Israel's way of life. Instead of a bond of covenant allegiance and devotion to the God of Egypt and Sinai, a new order of life emerged similar to that of the other west Asiatic kingships. Yet the situation was not quite so unambiguous, for the king was a charismatic person, the Anointed of the Lord. The Davidic king was the servant of Yahweh, the chosen and consecrated messiah, the representative and vicegerent of the Lord, who lived under the contingency of obedience and disobedience. It is clear, too, that the order of the covenant influenced the kingship of the dynasty of David (I Sam. 12) . Nevertheless, the kingdom had its own independent political development. It was a state among other western Asiatic states. The king entered into diplomatic relations, forged alliances, and joined his military forces with those of other nations. Political expediency became his primary concern. He ruled at his own discretion. Swept along by the currents of international events, Israel's history became inextricably bound with that of other peoples and increasingly took on their ways and ideologies. The secular kingship pre-empted the political, economic, and international fields. The old statutes and provisions of the Covenant Code were forgotten. The religions of the other peoples with their emphasis upon life, prosperity, and fertility held a great attraction for Israel. Yahweh and Baal became confused with each other; by whatever name they might call him, Yahweh often became to all intents and purposes another Baal.

The prophets raised their voices in protest against the new

order. They asserted Yahweh's rule over Israel. They defended his claim to be Israel's true Sovereign. They sought to perpetuate the ancient teachings regarding the relations of a man to his neighbor, Yahweh's justice over against the profitable alternatives imported from outside. Their verdict upon the kings is succinctly stated in the Deuteronomic pronouncement on nearly all of the kings, all except those who instituted movements of restoration and reformation: *"he did that which was evil in the sight of the Lord."* So Elijah, when he is accused of being the troubler of Israel, can reply to Ahab: "I have not troubled Israel, but you have, and your father's house, because you have forsaken the commandments of the Lord and followed after the Baals" (I Kings 18:18). Amos stoutly rejects the warning of Amaziah the priest to quit prophesying and says that Jeroboam will die by the sword (Amos 7:10-17). Isaiah states the alternatives between political expediency and faith in God in the sharpest terms; we hear again the ancient Either-Or of faith and infidelity, of allegiance and rebellion, and the unequivocal words of judgment: "If you will not believe, surely you shall not be established" (Isa. 7:9b; *see* Isa. 7:1-17). Again and again we have the scene before us of the prophet facing the king, speaking to him for Yahweh and reminding him of the higher sovereignty that rules over all kings and lords and potentates. The kings are judged and are found wanting.

It is the prophet Hosea, almost more than any other, who stands in intimate relation with the old covenant faith, and it is he who is most virulent in his condemnation of the kingship.

> Listen, O house of the king!
> For the judgment applies to you.
> Hosea 5:1b

Israel has forgotten its Maker and has built palaces, and Judah has multiplied its fortified cities, but Yahweh will send fire upon them (Hos. 8:14). They have deeply corrupted themselves, as in the days of Gibeah, the home of Saul (Hos. 9:9). It is an evil time. All the kings have fallen, and none calls upon Yahweh, their covenant Lord (Hos. 7:7). Israel sets up kings, but they were not appointed by God (Hos. 8:4). The king makes treaties, enters into international engagements, now with Egypt, now with Assyria (Hos. 5:13), but "aliens devour his strength, and he does not know it" (Hos. 7:9). In Hosea we listen to the great imperatives, the great vocatives, the invectives and threats. And he confronts Israel with the old demands for an answer:

> What will you do on the day of appointed festival,
>   on the day of the feast of the Lord?
>
> Hosea 9:5

The prophet is God's watchman over Israel (Hos. 9:8).

The invectives and threats resound through the other prophecies too, the same "woes" and irrevocable "therefores."

> "Woe to the rebellious children," says the Lord,
>   "who carry out a plan, but it is not mine;
> who make a league, but not of my spirit,
>   that they may add sin to sin. . . .
> Therefore shall the protection of Pharaoh turn to your shame,
>   and the shelter of the shadow of Egypt to your humiliation."
>
> Isaiah 30:1, 3

All treaties and alliances, all international relationships, all policies for national defense are under the judgment of the Lord of history, the transcendent King and Judge, who is solicitous for his people's well-being:

> Woe to those who go down to Egypt for help
>   and rely upon horses,
> who trust in chariots because they are many,
>   and in horsemen because they are strong,
> but do not look to the Holy One of Israel
>   or consult the Lord!
> And yet he is wise and brings disaster,
>   he does not call back his words,
> but will arise against the house of evil-doers,
>   and against the helpers of those who work iniquity.
>
> Isaiah 31:1-2

2. *The economic order.* Political and economic life are closely interrelated. A new political order influenced the eco-

nomic life of the people. Changing political situations affected their economic welfare. With the passing of the old seminomadic culture and the rise of the monarchy, new factors inevitably entered into Israel's life. Especially in the period of the Aramean wars in the ninth century and of the alliance with Phoenicia a radical alteration took place. Phoenician mercantilism invaded the royal court and Israelite society. The roots of the conflict between Israel and Aram were economic. They concerned the trade routes and international highways. A capitalistic class arose in Israel, and society became increasingly urban. This meant a revolution in Israel's way of life. Gone were the memories of the old sacral order, of the Teaching with its categorical demands for justice to the defenseless, of the higher loyalty transcending all other loyalties. Personal profit, unhampered and unchecked by higher considerations, drove the merchants and the leaders to new enterprises; the rich and the clever became insatiate in their greed for gain. Classes became stratified, and the rift between them ever more rigid and inflexible. With the loss of the old restraints we now hear of commercial dishonesty, exploitation of the poor, the luxury of the rich, gross indulgence, and insensate lust for profit.

Amidst all the feverish preoccupation with riches and power and comfort and pleasure; all the bustling commercial activity and the ever-rising prices; the building of fortifications for defense and of fine houses for the privileged; the elaboration of cultic observances with their sumptuous festivals and celebrations, their pilgrimages and rites, their music and choirs, and, withal, the syncretism with the cults of nature and prosperity—amidst all there was one voice that was stifled and repressed. It was the voice of Israel's covenant-making and covenant-keeping God. But was it stilled? Not quite! For there were prophets in the land to sound the cry of protest and outrage, repeating with the urgency born of faith and memory and holy awe, God's categorical and insistent "thou shalt not." The prophets called Israel to the way of hearing, the emphatic imperatives and the direct address:

Hear this, you who trample upon the needy!

Amos 5:4a

Hear, you heads of Jacob and rulers of the house of Jacob!

Micah 3:1

Again the invectives and threats, one following irrevocably upon the other:

> Therefore because you trample upon the poor
>   and take from him exactions of wheat,
> you have built houses of hewn stone,
>   but you shall not dwell in them;
> you have planted pleasant vineyards,
>   but you shall not drink their wine.
> For I know how many are your transgressions,
>   and how great are your sins—
> you who afflict the righteous, who take a bribe,
>   and turn aside the needy in the gate.

Amos 5:11-12

Woe to those who lie upon beds of ivory,
  and stretch themselves upon their couches,
and eat lambs from the flock,
  and calves from the midst of the stall;
who sing idle songs to the sound of the harp,
  and like David invent for themselves instruments of music;
and drink wine in bowls,
  and anoint themselves with the finest oils,
  but are not grieved over the ruin of Joseph!
Therefore they shall now be the first of those to go into exile,
  and the revelry of those who stretch themselves
  shall pass away.

Amos 6:4-7

The prophets are one in their judgments upon the moral delinquencies of their age, even so priestly a prophet as Ezekiel with his numerous cultic admonitions. In him we hear again the divine conditional:

> If the wicked restores the pledge, gives back what he has taken by robbery, and walks in the statutes of life, committing no iniquity, he shall surely live, he shall not die.

Ezekiel 33:15

The prophets remember God's first person self-asseverations and base their demands for honesty and justice upon them, precisely as in the teachings of the ancient sacral union at Sinai and Shechem:

> A trader, in whose hands are false balances,
>   he loves to oppress.
> Ephraim said, "Ah, but I am rich,
>   I have gained wealth for myself";
> but all his riches can never offset
>   the guilt he has incurred.
> I am the Lord your God
>   from the land of Egypt.
>
> Hosea 12:7-9a

Again there are the transcendent questions upon Israel's life:

> Shall I acquit the man with wicked scales
> and with a bag of deceitful weights?
>
> Micah 6:11

Throughout the centuries, in late literature as well as in early, the categorical, apodictic demands are repeated, restated, and augmented. Ezekiel incorporates them in the ecclesiastical community of the future:

> You shall have just balances, a just ephah, and a just bath.
>
> Ezekiel 45:10

The prophets cover the whole gamut of Israel's economic life. They have walked through the narrow lanes and streets of the city, they have listened to the bargainings at the bazaars, they have watched the poor make their pathetic little purchases and wait intently to see what their meager earnings will buy, they have seen the poor eating their pitiful fare of olives and bread, they have looked on the faces of anxiety and half-despair, and then they have observed the privileged, the powerful, the economically shrewd, and the professional leaders in league with one another to perpetuate the injustices and inequities of the urban mercantile economy, the capitalism of foreign importation. In the name of God they proclaim that this must not be. This must not be because God has a claim upon his people, upon all members of the social order who have the same access to him. There must be no poverty. The rights of the defenseless must be maintained in his name. No son of the covenant, no widow or orphan or resident foreigner, no one must be deprived of his inalienable rights. Whatever defense might be made for the legitimacy of the new economic system, whether of efficiency or of productivity or of national prestige or of maintaining one's place in the world of nations, all this is secondary to the divine concern for the individual, for the little man, the weak, and the disinherited. Material culture must be subjected to God's economy.

3. *Land.* Land is the primary basis of wealth. A people has often been defined in terms of its occupancy of a specific territory. Land and people surely are related, and in many significant ways. In the ancient Near East generally, the gods are bound to the soil. A mysterious bond unites them; the life-giving forces hidden in the soil are understood as the forces of fertility and life in the gods, and the people somehow share mysteriously in that secret. Thus the sexual life of the individual is related to the forces of reproduction within the soil. In Israel, however, the relation is conceived differently. There was nothing in the whole ancient world to compare to this understanding. The land is the gift of Yahweh, the Lord of history, to his people. It is the land promised to the fathers. The whole Yahwist epic moves forward to the time when Israel will occupy the land as its possession. It is a unique land, not like Egypt, for example, but "a land which Yahweh your God cares for; the eyes of Yahweh your God are always upon it, from the beginning of the year to the end of the year" (Deut. 11:12; cf. Deut. 8:7-10). Jeremiah speaks of Palestine as the most beautiful of all lands (Jer. 3:19).

But what is significant is that the land is given to Israel as Yahweh's heritage; it is given to her *provisionally;* it is under the same conditional as all other areas of Israel's existence. Fundamental to all biblical understanding of the land is the divine Word, recorded in a relatively late context but implicit in Israel's faith from earliest times: "The land belongs to me" (Lev. 25:23). Israel can never claim absolute possession of it.

Yahweh is its true owner, and Israelites are but sojourners and strangers in the land (Lev. 25:23). There is no *Blut und Boden* in the Old Testament; the whole faith militates against such a corruption. Yahweh is Lord of the land, and the land must respond to his bidding and indeed to his judgment (Amos 4:6-11). The radicalism of the ethical imperative is seen in the fact that the social transgressions of the people affect the productivity of the soil. The soil is corrupted by man's irresponsibility. The rights of the community to the land transcend the rights of the individual. This is not meant to say that private possession is condemned. Quite the contrary. Yahweh protects and upholds the possession of the poor farmer, for example, or of a man like Naboth. Not even Ahab the king, however just and considerate his proposition may seem to be, can take the land away from Naboth by force. Upon Ahab rests God's "thou shalt not" (I Kings 21).

The divine generosity is manifested in the gifts of fertility to the land. Not Baal, lord of the rain and the underground waters, but Yahweh, the God of history, determines whether the soil shall yield its produce:

> And she did not know
>   that it was I who gave her
> the grain, the wine, and the oil.
>
> Hosea 2:8a

And in a late passage:

> And in that day, says the Lord,
>   I will answer the heavens
>   and they shall answer the earth;
> and the earth shall answer the grain,
>   the wine, and the oil,
> and they shall answer Jezreel;
>   and I will sow him for myself in the land.
>
> Hosea 2:21-23a

Nature is under the jurisdiction of its Creator and Lord; like Israel, it too must respond in obedience and service to his will. The productivity of the land is determined by the conduct of those who inhabit it, for both land and people live under a common historical and moral sovereignty. When God commands it to yield, the land breaks forth into fertility and abundance; when he pronounces judgment upon it, it lies barren and desolate, and all that it has to yield is thorns and thistles.

Again the conditional preserves the covenantal contingency:

> If you are willing and obedient,
>   you shall eat the good of the land;
> But if you refuse and rebel,
>   you shall be devoured by the sword;
> for the mouth of the Lord has spoken.
>
> Isaiah 1:19-20; Jeremiah 7:24

The boundaries between nature and history are not so tightly drawn as we are accustomed to draw them, and for good reason. Both are under the rule of the same Ruler, both are created to serve a common purpose, both are the sphere of man's activity. The earth is the place for man to dwell in, the home in which man's history moves under the behest and reign of God, whose activity and will are determined by the way in which man assumes or rejects his responsibility.

The prophets betray extraordinary sensitiveness to the land, for they know to whom it belongs and are aware of the nature of Israel's relationship to it. Listen to Isaiah's invective!

> Woe to those who join house to house,
>   who add field to field,
> until there is no more room,
>   and you are made to dwell alone
>   in the midst of the land.
> The Lord of hosts has sworn in my hearing:
> "Surely many houses shall be desolate,
>   large and beautiful homes without inhabitant.
> For ten acres of vineyard shall yield but one bath,
>   and a homer of seed shall yield but an ephah."
>
> Isaiah 5:8-10

In a remarkable judicial encounter, Jeremiah can summarize Israel's whole past in terms of the land, and in doing so he portrays the appallment of the natural phenomena at Israel's irresponsibility and apostasy:

> They did not say, "Where is the Lord
>   who brought us up from the land of Egypt,
> who led us in the wilderness,
>   in a land of deserts and pits,
> in a land of drought and deep darkness,
>   in a land that none passes through,
>   where no man dwells."
> And I brought you into a plentiful land
>   to enjoy its fruits and its good things.
> But when you came in you defiled my land,
>   and made my heritage an abomination.
>
> Be appalled, O heavens, at this,
>   be shocked, be utterly desolate, says the Lord,
> for my people have committed two evils;
>   they have forsaken me,
> the fountain of living waters,
>   and hewed out cisterns for themselves,
> broken cisterns,
>   that can hold no water.
>
> Jeremiah 2:6-7, 12-13

4. *The administration of justice.* We are not so fully informed about Israel's courts of judgment as we might wish,[4] but the Old Testament has numerous references to the litigations that took place at the gate, where the elders judged and the people participated in the proceedings. We have seen how, in the Covenant Code, the divine demand is made for equal justice for all Israelites, whatever their class or status, and how the Deuteronomic Code elaborates and intensifies this demand for absolute impartiality. Here we see reflected the new conditions which arose in Israel as a result of the urban economy and the capitalistic drives for wealth and property.

The prophets are merciless in their condemnations of the misuse of judicial power. The courts have come under the

---

[4] But see the account in Ludwig Koehler, *Hebrew Man*, Appendix on "Justice in the Gate," (London: 1956).

control of the privileged and powerful, the rich and prosperous, the successful and aristocratic elements in the population.
As the king was reminded that he was subject to a higher sovereignty, so the judges are told that there is a Judge who judges
them. Landlord, patrician, priest, great and small, all share
a common obligation; all stand before the same ultimate judgment. We listen again to the ancient cry in behalf of the
weak and defenseless. In the laments we sense the grief of the
prophets at man's tyranny over man:

> Woe is me! For I have become
>   as when the summer fruit has been gathered,
>   as when the vintage has been gleaned:
> there is no cluster to eat,
>   no first-ripe fig which I desire.
> The godly man has perished from the earth,
>   and there is none upright among men;
> they all lie in wait for blood,
>   and each hunts his brother with a net.
> Their hands are upon what is evil,
>   to do it diligently;
> the prince and the judge ask for a bribe,
>   and the great man utters the evil desire of his soul;
>   thus they weave it together.
>
> Micah 7:1-3

This incessant and insatiable greed for gain is one of the recurring themes of prophetic protest. But what is even worse
is that the judges acquit the guilty for a bribe and deprive the
innocent of their rights (Isa. 5:23; Mic. 7:3; Ezek. 22:12; etc.).
Jeremiah excoriates the king for refusing to pay his laborers
their just wages (Jer. 22:13).

There were those, of course, who sought to circumvent the
demands of justice by fabricating a network of legislation in
which they might enmesh the guileless and innocent. Isaiah
denounces those who decree iniquitous decrees and the paid
scribes who keep writing oppressive laws in order to exploit
the needy and the poor, and calls them to God's accounting:

> What will you do on the day of punishment,
>   in the storm which will come from afar?

To whom will you flee for help,
and where will you leave your wealth?

                                        Isaiah 10:3

The prophets' words are vehement in their outrage, almost
brutal in their outspokenness. They show little regard for the
niceties of convention. They are scandalized by what is going
on. When one considers that some of them at least came from
respected families, men like Isaiah and Jeremiah and Ezekiel,
it is shocking to hear them exposing to the view of everyone
what the "important" people are doing to the "little" people.
But they can speak as they do because they speak in the name
of the righteous Judge (Jer. 12:1), who tolerates no partiality,
who is grieved for the poor and the weak, and who makes no
distinction between one man and another. To all who exploit
others and take advantage of their power and wealth, he addresses the same passionate question: "What do you mean by
treating your brother in this way?"

5. *Power and pride.* In all this we witness one of the most
striking and one of the most pervasive features of the prophetic
polemic: the denunciation and distrust of power in all its
forms and guises. The hunger of the powerful knows no satiety;
the appetite grows on what it feeds. Power exalts itself and
is incapable of yielding to any transcendent judgment; it
"listens to no voice" (Zeph. 3:2). It is something much more
than an idealizing of the nomadic past or a utopian dream of
an ideal social order which accounts for the prophetic scorn
and disdain of the strong and privileged. Here, too, we see
the effects of the covenant way of life. It is astonishing to observe how little deference the prophets show to the kings. Con-
sidering that the king was the Lord's Anointed and his chosen
representative, it is surprising to hear them address him in the
most downright and relentless fashion. Like the historians, they
give the successful kings less than their due; indeed, it is precisely *they* who are often under the deepest suspicion. The
prophets give too little heed to the real political and international problems with which the state is confronted, the necessity for political alliances and national defense, the inevitable
compromises in a world of power politics, or the radical tensions between national policy and religious faith.

All that is strong falls under the prophetic lash. There is the city which becomes oppressive, which magnifies itself, dwells securely and says to itself, "I am and there is none else" (Zeph. 2:15) . The mark of Cain, its first founder (Gen. 4:17) , is upon it. The sins of the nation are the sins of its cities (Mic. 1:5) . All the professions are subjected to the same acid criticism: priests, prophets, scribes and sages, princes, and judges. They are all tempted to abuse their power and status and to become victims to their pride. Even women, especially the wives of the rich, are bitterly denounced for their haughtiness and heartlessness. The prophets show little chivalry; the modern ideal of the gentleman is not to be found in the Old Testament. Amos can condemn the rich women of his time with a rigor that makes one wince (Amos 4:1-3) , and even the courtly Isaiah shows no hesitation in describing them in most realistic terms:

> The Lord said:
> Because the daughters of Zion are haughty
> and walk with outstretched necks,
> glancing wantonly with their eyes,
> mincing as they go,
> tinkling with their feet:
> the Lord will smite with a scab
> the heads of the daughters of Zion,
> and the Lord will lay bare their secret parts.
>
> Isaiah 3:16-17; cf. 3:18-24

We should hardly expect Isaiah of all the prophets to speak in this way.

But there is more. Yahweh is *against* all those things which we should characterize as the inevitable marks of civilization:

> For the Lord has a day
> against all that is proud and lofty,
> against all that is lifted up and high;
> against all the cedars of Lebanon,
> lofty and lifted up;
> and against all the oaks of Bashan;
> against all the high mountains,
> and against all the lofty hills;
> against every high tower,

> and against every fortified wall;
> against all the ships of Tarshish,
>   and against all the beautiful craft.
> And the haughtiness of man shall be humbled,
>   and the pride of men shall be brought low;
>   and the Lord alone will be exalted in that day.
>
> Isaiah 2:12-17

The mighty empires—Babylon, Assyria, Egypt, and the rest
—come within the range of prophetic scorn and disdain. In
the eighth century B.C., the Assyrian king becomes God's instrument of judgment against Israel, but the king boasts of his own
unaided victories:

> By the strength of my hand I have done it,
>   and by my wisdom, for I have understanding.
>
> Isaiah 10:13a

He, too, is confronted with the divine interrogative:

> Shall the ax vaunt itself over him who hews with it,
>   or the saw magnify itself against him who wields it?
> As if a rod should wield him who lifts it,
>   or as if a staff should lift him who is not wood!
>
> Isaiah 10:15

The kings make gods of themselves, they exult in their wisdom
and knowledge, they are guilty of the cardinal sin of *hybris*. At
the heyday of her power, Chaldea boasts, "I shall be mistress
for ever"; she shows no mercy, never gives thought for a moment to what she is doing or remembers the end. She sits secure in her wickedness and says "No one is seeing me"; her
knowledge and wisdom leads her astray, and she says to herself,
"I am, and there is no one beside me." But such a claim belongs only to God (Isa. 47:5-10). The prince of Tyre, too, is
arrogant in his claims to infallibility; he considers himself
wise as a god, and he luxuriates in her vast wealth.

> Because your heart is proud,
>   and you have said, "I am a god,
> I sit in the seat of the gods,

in the heart of the seas,"
yet you are but a man, and no god,
    though you consider yourself wise as a god. . . .
therefore, behold, I will bring strangers upon you,
    the most terrible of the nations.

                                                Ezekiel 28:2, 7a

The vaunting pride and arrogance of the mighty will be brought low by the Lord of history. There is a monition which keeps interposing itself throughout the Scriptures: *Be not proud!*

Talk no more so very proudly,
    let not arrogance come from your mouth;
For the Lord is a God of knowledge,
    and by him actions are weighed.

                                I Samuel 2:13; cf. Jeremiah 13:15-17

Nowhere in the Old Testament is this motif of the tyranny of the strong expressed so movingly as in Ezekiel's great allegory of the shepherds and their flocks. The shepherd is the symbol for the king, as it is generally throughout the ancient Near East. The prophet indicts the rulers:

Ho, shepherds of Israel who have been feeding yourselves! Should not shepherds feed the sheep?

                                                Ezekiel 34:2b

The indictment continues:

The weak you have not strengthened, the sick you have not healed, the crippled you have not bound up, the strayed you have not brought back, the lost you have not sought, and with force and harshness you have ruled them.

                                                Ezekiel 34:4

So the sheep are scattered because there was no shepherd. But the time of accounting comes:

Thus says the Lord God, "Behold I am against the shepherds; and I will require my sheep at their hand."

                                                Ezekiel 34:10a

This passage is notable in itself, but what makes it even more significant is that it strikes a chord that is heard from the earliest times in ancient Israel. God is solicitous and active in behalf of the weak. The defenseless are his special concern. He sends his messengers to defend their rights. So the prophets are always on the alert where justice is at stake. They are not impressed by the power and prosperity of the privileged; indeed, they pour the vials of divine wrath upon them because they use their prerogatives for their own ends. They are not impressed by ostentation and bigness. They are not carried away by the clamant voices of politicians in the royal courts, traders in the market places, professional optimists on the street corners, or by the wise men with their too simple counsels, nor are they much moved by the passions of the vocal majorities.

They listen to the waters of Shiloah that flow softly and put their trust in them. They suffer the absence of God, but know by that knowledge which faith gives that the future is in his hands. The waters of the Euphrates "mighty and many" will engulf those who seek security in them, and will bring them to ruin (Isa. 8:5-8). The king is strong in his compassion and solicitude (Isa. 32:1-8), he is weak when his power tempts him to arrogance, self-sufficiency, and tyranny. Man's history belongs to God, and man is responsible to God for the way he lives in it.

6. *The world of nations.* Israel enters upon the stage of world history in an international age. In many ways she was related to the other peoples of the ancient Near East. She belonged to the Semitic family of peoples and shared much in common with them. The history of the great empires and of the smaller nations—above all, of Assyria, Chaldea, Egypt, and Phoenicia—exercised an influence upon her own history. Her literature exhibits many similarities to the literatures of her neighbors, especially in her poetry, but also in her law and Wisdom. Even in her religion she borrowed extensively, notably in her cultic observances and rituals. Throughout her history, Israel was deeply involved in the way of the nations. Without some grasp of the international relations of Israel, it is impossible to understand the words of the historians and prophets.

Yet, over against the frequent references to Israel's involvement with the other peoples of the ancient Near East, there is another witness to her uniqueness and her separation from them. In the divinations of Balaam, emanating in all likelihood from the period of David, she is described as "a people dwelling alone, not reckoning itself among the nations" (Num. 23:9), and in the moving dialogue in which Moses asks to see the divine glory he pleads, "Is it not in thy going with us, so that we are distinct, I and thy people, from all other people that are upon the face of the earth?" (Exod. 33:16). It is precisely this awareness of being set apart for a destiny that pervades the literature of Israel, and it was only natural that the history of the world should therefore be viewed from the standpoint of the centrality of a people chosen to fulfill the divine purpose in history. The hill of Zion becomes "the holy mountain, beautiful in elevation, the joy of all the earth" (Ps 48:2), toward which all the peoples go to worship Yahweh (Isa. 11:10; Jer. 16:19).

The fate of the nations of the world is viewed in different ways by different prophets, depending in part upon the historical situation, in part upon the world-view of the particular prophet. In some contexts, they are to be destroyed, especially on the Day of Yahweh, the Day of the divine triumph and accounting; but prophets like Amos and Isaiah could contradict popular optimistic expectations by including Israel within the judgment (Amos 5:18-20; Isa. 2:6-19). In other contexts, the nations are to experience the judgment of Yahweh that they may know that he alone is God, that he alone is Sovereign in history, that Israel may be vindicated before their eyes, and that they may realize that there is a God who is working out his purpose among men. Sometimes, too, God uses the nations as the instruments of his wrath against the chosen and covenanted people, against "a godless nation," though they may not be aware of it and may in reality corrupt their divine mission on the earth.

What is noteworthy, however, is that for men like the writer of the Yahwist epic, Amos, Isaiah, and Second Isaiah, they are brought within the horizon of the covenanted people. The justice and mercy and love of God could not for them be confined to one people only, for that would be neither justice nor mercy nor love, but must assert its gracious sovereignty among other peoples as well. The grace of God in prophets like Amos,

Isaiah, Second Isaiah, and some of the anonymous writers em-
braces all peoples and races, even the most bitter of Israel's
enemies. Nations will come to see the light of Israel and will
bring to her gifts of gold and frankincense, and will proclaim
the name of Yahweh in the new-found joy of adoration (Isa.
60:1 ff.) . They will confess that Yahweh is with Israel and will
learn that it is to her that he has committed the keeping of the
Torah; so they wait in glad anticipation for its guidance and
direction and revelation (Isa. 42:1-4). The promise of the
blessing made to Abraham will be fulfilled, and the princes of
the earth will gather together as the people of the God of Abraham (cf. Ps. 47) .

In a series of oracles with similar form and structure, Amos
launches his invectives and threats against the nations of his
time, especially those with whom Israel's recent history had
been closely connected (Amos 1:3-2:16) . Here the divine rule
extends far beyond the confines of Palestine. It determines the
course that history takes in all of these nations. God's will determines the future of each of them. All the nations stand
under a common sovereignty and a common judgment. Yet the
divine compassion is also reflected in these oracles of judgment.
It is an appalling thing that Moab should burn the bones of
the king of Edom to lime (Amos 2:1) . Tyre did not remember
the covenant of brothers (Amos 1:9b) . Gaza carried into exile
a whole people! (Amos 1:6) . This is what nations can do and
do do to each other. That is the power they have. But a nation's
offense against nation is defiance of God. It is his power, not
theirs, that is decisive. Their instruments of war will avail them
nothing in the time of accounting. Amos goes further and pro-
claims that Israel is under the same transcendent historical
judgment as the other peoples, with most of whom she has
waged bitter conflict. Indeed, the oracles culminate in the long
and bitter denunciation of the chosen people. It must be remembered as we listen to these impassioned arraignments that
they are spoken, not as the private protests of Amos himself, but
as God's words. So it is all the more impressive that they should
so abound with historical detail, a stirring witness to the seri-
ousness with which God takes history and to the way that Israel
was also called to take it.

The consequences of the prophetic view of history implied

in these oracles are of course momentous. Amos cuts straight through the distortion and corruption of the election and covenant relationships by their nationalistic interpretations.

> You only have I known
>   of all the families of the earth;
> therefore I will punish you
>   for all your iniquities.

Amos 3:2

In the eyes of the majority, this would seem to be an utter *non sequitur;* on the contrary, says Amos, it exposes the inner "logic" of the original bond. Israel has renounced the responsibilities of election, therefore she will suffer the consequences inherent in it. Amos sounds the death-knell of nationalism.

> "Are you not like the Ethiopians to me,
>   O people of Israel?" says the Lord.
> "Did I not bring up Israel from Egypt?" says the Lord.

Amos 9:7a

Every Israelite would assent to that, for it marked the beginning of Israel's history. But then the prophet continues:

> and the Philistines from Caphtor
> and the Syrians from Kir?

Amos 9:7b

That was quite another matter. The doors to universalism have been thrown wide. Amos is saying that the Philistines and Syrians have had their Exodus too! How far would he press the implications of these divine events?

But if we are to view the more spacious ranges of the prophetic understanding of history, it is to Isaiah of Jerusalem, above all others perhaps, that we should turn. He stands at one of the junctures of world history, midstream in the career of the Assyrian empire, and much of what he has to say is directed to the international situation. Assyria has its imperialistic designs and plans, which involved the subjugation of all the peoples standing in the path of her aggressions. But over

against these plans is the plan of which the Assyrians had taken
no account:

> The Lord of hosts has sworn:
> "As I have planned,
>   so shall it be,
> and as I have purposed,
>   so shall it stand,
> that I will break the Assyrian in my land,
>   and upon my mountains trample him under foot."
>
> Isaiah 14:24-25a

The earth belongs to God, and history belongs to him. Yet he
can use the Assyrians against his own people, "a godless nation." But nothing of the sort was in the mind of the conqueror.
He boasts of his own conquests, his power and wisdom, his ability to gather all the nations under his sway. So he, too, must
face the divine questioning:

> Shall the ax vaunt itself over him who hews with it?
>
> Isaiah 10:15a

The meaning of world history is to be understood in the light
of a transcendent plan overarching and penetrating all human
plans and bringing them to nought.

Isaiah is also saying that there is a Providence that watches
over history and that Israel may rely upon the unseen guiding
hand. If they will not have faith, they will not be established
(Isa. 7:7). Yahweh has laid in Zion a precious cornerstone, a
sure foundation: "He who believes will not be in haste," for
justice is the line, and righteousness the plummet (Isa.
28:16-17). With such confidence in the providential ordering of
history and the ultimate vindication of the divine purpose,
Isaiah can portray the nations streaming to Jerusalem to go to
the house of the God of Israel "that he may teach us his ways,
and that we may walk in his paths":

> For out of Zion shall go forth the law,
>   and the word of God from Jerusalem.
> He shall judge between the nations,

> and shall decide for many peoples;
> and they shall beat their swords into plowshares,
>   and their spears into pruning hooks;
> nation shall not lift up sword against nation,
>   neither shall they learn war any more.
>
> Isaiah 2:3b-4; cf. Micah 4:1-5

Amos and Isaiah had their successors, who could speak much in the same manner. One of them, whose words are preserved for us in Isaiah, looks forward to the time when the consequences of their universalism will be drawn:

> In that day there will be a highway from Egypt to Assyria, and the Assyrian will come into Egypt, and the Egyptian into Assyria, and the Egyptians will worship with the Assyrians.
> In that day Israel will be a third with Egypt and Assyria, a blessing in the midst of the earth, whom the Lord of hosts has blessed, saying, "Blessed be Egypt my people, and Assyria the work of my hands, and Israel my heritage."
>
> Isaiah 19:23-24; cf. Psalm 87:4-6

The writer of the little book of Jonah also knows that the Assyrians are men, and come within the range of the divine compassion and forgiveness. On the other hand, the prophets know that the nations are also under judgment:

> Multitudes, multitudes,
>   in the valley of decision!
> For the day of the Lord is near
>   in the valley of decision.
> The sun and the moon are darkened,
>   and the stars withdraw their shining.
>
> Joel 3:14-15

THE WAY OF THE WISE MEN

When we turn from the prophets to the wise men of ancient Israel, we find ourselves in the presence of teachers and counselors with quite another mood and cast of mind. Here, if anywhere, we may speak with some propriety of ethics, at least in an elemental form. We may legitimately ask the question,

"What does it mean to be good or just or wise or happy?" for many passages will give us an answer which is clear and intelligible. The sources of Israel's Wisdom do not lie in the events of the sacred past as they do with the prophets and the psalmists of Israel; there is no reference anywhere to the election, the covenant, or even to the Torah. Where Torah is mentioned, as it often is, it is (with one exception) not the divinely given teaching. Rather, the sources of the Wisdom literature are to be discerned in the international Wisdom of the ancient Near Eastern world, notably Egypt and Edom and possibly the Wisdom of the desert. In one instance, we now have the original lying behind the biblical text, namely, the Proverbs of Amenemope, which are reproduced in Proverbs 22:17-24:22. Other sections of Proverbs show striking connections with Egyptian Wisdom, sometimes word for word.

Yet it is a mistake to regard Israel's Wisdom literature as an aberrant bloc in the Old Testament. Its oldest strata are very early, probably anteceding the reign of Solomon, who came to be regarded as the wise man par excellence. Little of the literature that has been ascribed to him is in reality his, but this must not be taken to deny the accuracy of the tradition that he was a maker of proverbs and maxims, and it may well be that at least some of those given in the Old Testament belong to him. But more than that, Wisdom runs its course throughout the history of Israel's literature and extends into the apocrypha and pseudepigrapha, and beyond them into the New Testament and rabbinical writings. This Wisdom belongs to Israel, and while much of it is borrowed, it again and again bears the authentic stamp of the people. If one regards Proverbs as a whole, for example, it is apparent that the collections have been assembled from a dominating point of view, that it is Yahweh who gives wisdom, and that it is from him that knowledge and understanding proceed (Prov. 2:6). The fear of Yahweh is the beginning both of knowledge (Prov. 1:7) and of wisdom, and the knowledge of the Holy One is insight (Prov. 9:10). The discipline to which one is subjected is Yahweh's (Prov. 3:11). We are told that it is Yahweh who weighs the spirit (Prov. 16:2) or the heart, the seat of the will (Prov. 21:2; cf. 24:12), although both the idea and the terminology is derived from the Egyptian source. Prophecy has left its impress in some contexts, and it is worth observing that many of the concerns of both lawgiver and prophet are shared by the sages. Here, too, it is necessary to be cautious, for often there are close affinities with foreign Wisdom where we should be least inclined to expect them.

Like the Deuteronomists and the prophets, the wise men of Israel range over the whole of life and society. The relations of parent and child, husband and wife, king and subject, teacher and pupil, friend and friend, employer and employee, and others are examined, often with remarkable perspicuity. We are given much sage counsel, shrewd observation, even penetrating insight. The wise man is not a pedestrian moralist. He does not possess the fire and passion of the prophet, he does not soar so high on the wings of imagination or descend so deep (except possibly in Job) into the depths of pain and suffering. His temper is more subdued, more restrained, more conventional; his imagery more homespun, more secondhand. Everyday experience plays a greater role with him. He has learned from observation what he counsels others to do and not to do. At the same time, he sees the value of discipline, integrity, charity, and prudence. He tends to be conservative, even-tempered, and slightly academic.

The wise man counsels charity to the poor:

> He who is kind to the poor lends to the Lord.
> Proverbs 19:17a

> He who oppresses a poor man insults his Maker,
>   but he who is kind to the needy honors him.
> Proverbs 14:31

With his predecessors he is concerned for the orphan:

> Do not remove an ancient landmark
>   or enter the fields of the fatherless;
> for their Redeemer is strong;
>   he will plead their cause against you.
> Proverbs 23:10-11

A poor man who walks in integrity is better than a rich man who is perverse in his ways (Prov. 28:6) . A liberal man will be

the richer for his liberality (Prov. 11:24-26). While he sees no
harm in riches as such, he counsels against trusting in them
(Prov. 11:28) or making them an end:

> Do not toil to acquire wealth,
>   be wise enough to desist.
>
>   Proverbs 23:4

It is gone before one knows it (Prov. 23:5). He who hastens to
be rich will not go unpunished (Prov. 28:20b). On the other
hand:

> A good man leaves an inheritance,
>   to his children's children,
> but the sinner's wealth is laid up
>   for the righteous.
>
>   Proverbs 13:22

There are things more important in life than possessions:

> He who pursues righteousness and kindness
>   will find life and honor. [cf. Hebrew: "life
>   and righteousness"]
>
>   Proverbs 21:21

The ancient demands for social justice and the prophetic protests are echoed in his words:

> A just balance and scales belong to the Lord;
>   all the weights in the bag are his work.
>
>   Proverbs 16:11

He asserts laconically but pregnantly the basic *sine qua nihil:*
Partiality in judging is not good (Prov. 24:23; cf. Prov. 18:5;
28:21; Ps. 82:2).

The ancient Hebrew was not an ascetic. He enjoyed eating
and drinking and the other pleasures of life. But one can
overdo it.

> He who loves pleasure will be a poor man;
>   he who loves wine and oil will not be rich.
>
>   Proverbs 21:17

In such counsels as these, we recognize the great respect the sage had for the disciplines of life. He was not a fanatic, but he had a sense of values, and protested against extremes. Wine is good and food is good, but one should not be a winebibber or a glutton. He is close to the μηδὲν ἀγάν of the Greeks or to the *medium tenuere beati* of the Romans.

The sage had contempt for laziness, and by the same token a healthy respect for hard work. It is one of the most character-istic and constant of his themes:

> Go to the ant, thou sluggard;
>   consider her ways, and be wise.
> Without having any chief,
>   officer or ruler,
> she prepares her food in summer,
>   and gathers her sustenance in harvest.
> How long will you lie there, O sluggard:
>   when will you rise from your sleep?
> A little sleep, a little slumber,
>   a little folding of the hands to rest,
> and poverty will come upon you like a vagabond,
>   and want like an armed man.
>   Proverbs 6:6-11; cf. Proverbs 10:26;
>   12:11; 13:4; 15:19; 20:4; 24:30-34; 21:25; 26:16

Like the prophets, the wise men criticized pride, but in much more measured terms:

> When pride comes, comes disgrace;
>   but with the humble is wisdom.
>   Proverbs 11:2

> A man's pride will bring him low,
>   but he who is lowly in spirit will obtain honor.
>   Proverbs 29:23

The difference between the prophetic fulminations and sa-piential counsels measures the gap between the two, yet it must not be forgotten that behind all these moral counsels

and reflections is the motive of a genuine, if somewhat unim-
passioned, piety.

The pedagogic interests of the wise man are suggested in his
reflections upon various human relationships. The king must
be obeyed and proper deference shown him:

My son, fear the Lord and the king,
  and do not disobey either of them;
for disaster from them will rise suddenly,
  and who knows the ruin that will come from them both.
                                        Proverbs 24:21-22

A man should recognize his superiors. One wonders what an
Amos or a Micah would have had to say to that.

The solidarity of the family should be maintained:

He who troubles his family will inherit the wind,
  and a fool will be servant to the wise.
                                        Proverbs 11:29

The command of the Decalogue to honor one's father and
mother receives strong support, though it is by no means clear
that the wise man was thinking of it in his numerous admonitions to obedience and respect. He believed that children
should be administered corporal punishment:

Do not withhold discipline from a child;
  if you beat him with a rod, he will not die.
If you beat him with the rod,
  you will save his life from Sheol.
                        Proverbs 23:13-14; cf. Proverbs 19:18

There is the boy who hates discipline and despises reproof,
who does not listen to his teachers or pay attention to their
instruction, but it brings him to the brink of ruin (Prov.
5:12-14). The fool plays a role in the thinking of the sage.
He is always proclaiming his folly; how different from the
prudent man who "conceals knowledge" (Prov. 12:23). The
gossip is constantly telling secrets, but the trustworthy person
keeps his counsel (Prov. 11:13). The disciplined person doesn't
lose his temper:

A man of great wrath will pay the penalty;
    for if you deliver him you will only have to do it again.
                                        Proverbs 19:19, RSV

A soft answer turns away wrath,
    but a harsh word stirs up anger.
                                        Proverbs 15:1

He who is slow to anger is better than he who takes a city.
                                        Proverbs 16:32

One of the happier parts of the Wisdom teaching is the high value it places on friendship:

Your friend, and your father's friend, do not forsake;
    and do not go to your brother's house in the day of your calamity.
                                        Proverbs 27:10a, b

There are friends who pretend to be friends,
    but there is a friend who sticks closer than a brother.
                                        Proverbs 18:24

A man should have a good wife and be careful in choosing her. A quarrelsome woman is an abomination:

It is better to live in a corner of the housetop
    than in a house shared by a contentious woman.
                                Proverbs 21:9; cf. Proverbs 19:13; 27:15

The loose woman is the object of the wise man's scorn and ridicule; he knows both the lure and the peril of her ways, and he can be very realistic in describing her wiles (Prov. 7). On the other hand, the sage gives us a wonderful portrait of what he considers the ideal wife. It is worth pondering. She is not only industrious and efficient, but knows how to make her home beautiful, comfortable, and well provided. She is charitable, clever, and wise. She opens her hand to the poor, and reaches out her hand to the needy (Prov. 31:20). No wonder that

Her children rise up and call her blessed;
her husband also, and he praises her:
"Many women have done excellently,
but you surpass them all."

Proverbs 31:28-29

There is something authentic in such lines; one listens here as elsewhere throughout Proverbs to the voice of experience.

Noteworthy, too, are the counsels concerning the treatment of the enemy:

Do not rejoice when your enemy falls,
and let not your heart be glad when he stumbles;
lest the Lord see it and be displeased,
and turn away his anger from him.

Proverbs 24:17-18

One regrets the motivation of the prohibition, but there are other lines like the following:

Do not say, "I will do to him as he has done to me;
I will pay the man back for what he has done."

Proverbs 24:29

In the spirit of the early laws, but perhaps somewhat more advanced, one is admonished:

If your enemy is hungry, give him bread to eat;
and if he is thirsty, give him water to drink;
for you will heap coals of fire on his head,
and the Lord will reward you.

Proverbs 25:21; cf. Romans 12:20

It is possible that in one context we have a specific allusion to prophecy and law; if so, it affords us an interior glimpse into the mind and heart of the wise man:

Where there is no prophecy the people cast off restraint,
but blessed is he who keeps the law.

Proverbs 29:18

If these words are ambiguous, then we may rest more securely in a short prayer, which summarizes the mood of the wise man as we trace it in his words:

> Two things I ask of thee;
> deny them not to me before I die:
> Remove from me falsehood and lying;
> give me neither poverty nor riches;
> feed me with the food that is needful for me,
> lest I be full, and deny thee,
> and say, "Who is the Lord?"
> or lest I be poor, and steal,
> and profane the name of my God.
>
> Proverbs 30:7-9

5
The Way of Worship

WHEN WE UNDERTAKE TO INQUIRE WHAT IS THE
supreme good for man, the answer of the Old Testament is
plain for all to hear. It is supremely good for man to worship
God. In the priestly creation liturgy with which the Bible
opens (Gen. 1:1-2:4a), the whole universe—the heavens and
earth and all created things—is made subservient to time and
God's ordering of it. The world of space is subordinated to
the world of time. All the forces of life and vitality and fertility have their origin in the Word of God: "And God said."
But creation is also subjected to the sanctification of the day.
God blesses the seventh day and makes it holy. Later Jewish
writers were only developing what is implicit in the liturgy,
that the Sabbath was the purpose for the creation of the universe. Man was given a home and was created to sing his great
Creator's praise. Even the heavenly bodies know this, for they
keep proclaiming the story of their birth (Ps. 19).

No hymn was more familiar in Israel and none more frequently sung than the song of thanksgiving celebrating the
divine goodness (Ps. 136; cf. Pss. 106:1; 107:1; 118:1; 135:3;
II Chron. 7:3). It is good to sing praises to God (Ps. 92:1),
for praise becomes him (Ps. 147:1). The poets of Israel are
never at a loss to tell us why it is good to do so. They keep
recalling all the mighty works and the words which accompanied them. The divine goodness is revealed in the "historicity" of Israel and of the individual worshiper who belongs
to the holy community. The *magnalia* of Israel's past are present whenever she appears before the God who creates history,
attends it, directs it to its goal, and calls men to accountability
in it.

Worship is not a flight to "the dim Unknown," to timelessness, or to "a presence that disturbs me with the joy of ele-

vated thoughts," or to a shoreless ocean of quietude and unper-
turbed peace. Everywhere there is movement, active and ardent
speaking, and live response to the speaking and acting Lord.
Israel praises the King because his covenant love and faithfulness endure to all generations. She praises him because he
continues to do in the present hour what he did in the past.

> Father of the fatherless and protector of widows
>   is God in his holy habitation.
> God gives the desolate a home to dwell in;
>   he leads out the prisoners to prosperity;
>   but the rebellious dwell in a parched land.
>
> Psalm 68:5

Israel praises God because in her worship she is given direction and guidance for her way through history (Ps. 119:68).
It is therefore the chief of her joys to go to the sanctuary and
to tarry in its holy courts. There she may listen to the proclamation of the holy Name, there she may "seek his face," there
she may listen to priests and prophets speaking the words which
belong to the life that was peculiarly hers, and there she may
respond in adoration, confession, thanksgiving, and supplica-
tion to the God who first addressed her in the *magnalia*. The
sound of great joy is heard in the holy precincts:

> How lovely is thy dwelling place,
>   O Lord of hosts!
> My soul longs, yea, faints
>   for the courts of the Lord;
> my heart and my flesh sing for joy
>   to the living God.
>
> Psalm 84:1; cf. Psalms 26:8; 27:4

Worship is holy meeting. In worship, man enters into the
sphere of holiness, into the presence of the Holy One. Israel
was born in the hour of the covenant to be a holy nation or
people. In her worship she remembers God's self-witness, "I,
the Lord, am holy," and to it she responds confessionally, "The
Lord our God is holy" (Ps. 99). The holy life to which she is
called was bodied forth in the living encounter of words,

spoken and heard. Yahweh had met the patriarchs on the way
in awesome theophanies, and they had erected altars to preserve the memory of the event. But with the theophany, Yahweh
had called the fathers to an engagement in holy word and event.
At Sinai, he had met with Israel in the supreme theophany,
and there, too, he had entrusted her with words for her holy
keeping. In the cult, Israel remembers the holy past, and in
the spoken recital it becomes present, for in truth it was meant
for every present.

Yahweh gives the event and the accompanying word, and
in both there is the effectual power of his life-giving activity.
So the faithful Israelite goes to the ancient sanctuaries—to
Hebron, Bethel, Beersheba, Gilgal, Shechem, Shiloh, and the
others—for it was in these places that God had granted her
ancestors the assurance not only of his presence but of words
spoken for guidance and direction, in need and distress, in
hope and anticipation. But, in contrast to the religions of other
Near Eastern peoples, the place bore no sanctity in and of itself. What made it holy or sacred was the event in time. This
leads us to a major reflection upon Israel's faith: *it is not bound
to the world of space.* Yahweh is never limited to any locality,
however holy. He is not confined to the sanctuary (II Sam.
7:5-7; Ezek. 10:18 ff.).

In the Temple on Zion's holy hill, Yahweh causes his Name
to dwell, and it is there that the Name is given present reality
by being spoken and proclaimed, and there, too, that men
call on the Name and are answered. Not the Temple edifice
but the Holy Name is of first and central concern. Yahweh
manifests himself in the mystery of time and times, and it is
with these times that Israel has to do. These times which God
gives his people are for remembering, for rehearsing in living
words, for activating in cultic drama, and for joyous celebration. It is *good* for Israel to be granted this way of life.

The Invisible One Enthroned is active in the times allotted
to Israel. As One who reveals himself in events, he must not
be represented in spatial imagery. That would be to make of
him someone over whom one might dispose, an object which
one could in some way control or manage. Over this perennial
temptation to spatialize the Lord of history, the Bible is urgent
and emphatic in its categorical *"thou shalt not."* Israel cannot

see him, must not see him, for he is incomparable, transcendent, holy, and unbound. It is the greatness of Israel's faith that her God is invisible. So she is called from the beginning to walk by faith as Abraham her father had walked, with no other support, no other evidence or guarantee, than the Word spoken, the promise for the future. Israel lives in time and history, and because this is the destiny to which she has been called, the categorical imperative of *sola fide* is present on the way she treads.[1]

The Psalter is pre-eminently the Book of Prayer and Praise. Many of the songs, hymns, prayers, and laments have their setting in the cult, and they were employed in its exercise. It is seldom that we can be sure precisely what function they played in Israel's worship, and this is a grievous loss to us. For the psalms are not the product of human artifice and genius, but the modes of expression employed by Israel in all the various and manifold exigencies of daily life and historical existence, when she stood in the presence of her covenant-keeping Lord, who reigned as king on the royal throne of the ark sequestered in the little adytum of the royal sanctuary. In the Psalter, we listen to the way of Israel's speaking in the presence of the Holy One.

Notable among the features which mark this work of prayer and praise is the large place that is accorded the memorable events of the past. History is drawn into the sphere of the divine holiness. The holiness of God manifests itself in his

---

[1] To be sure, the motif of "seeing God" is frequently present in the Old Testament: in theophanies, in worship, and in ecstatic vision. Indeed, the Old Testament nowhere states that God is invisible. Such a generalization would be out of keeping with Israelite thought and speech. Several observations may be in order here: (1) the instances where God is said to be "seen" must be regarded as highly exceptional, beyond the ordinary ways in which God vouchsafes his presence for Israel; (2) in many instances we are manifestly dealing with borrowed cultic terminology, especially in the royal cult, which was profoundly influenced by Near Eastern cults; (3) even the theophanies and visions are very reserved in describing what is seen; they are notable for their want of portraiture; (4) in all the visions, even those of Ezekiel, the world of seeing passes imperceptibly into the world of hearing; one is not overawed by the transcendent spectacle but remembers the words spoken; (5) in the apocalypses, in contrast to the prophecies, the visual does assume a major role, but it is doubtful whether they may be said to represent the major movement of biblical faith; borrowing is plainly present here, too. The central affirmation, despite exceptions, still holds: "No man shall see me and live."

gracious deeds in Israel's history. The acts of God in creation are also hymned, to be sure; indeed, they stir Israel most spontaneously to singing and adoration. This is true of the literatures of the other peoples of the Ancient Near East. In style, form, and terminology, their hymns of creation are often not unlike those we have in Israel, but what is remarkable in the latter is that they are usually combined with the "wonderful deeds" of Israel's unique historical past. Nowhere in the whole Old Testament are the references to these mighty acts more frequent and indeed more inwardly appropriated than in the Psalter, and they appear in many different kinds of speaking, whether hymn or lament or thanksgiving or blessing or liturgy. It is more than a mere chronicling of events we have before us. The events are grasped as revelation, and revelation is a call to obedience and service and faithfulness and rejoicing. Psalm 78, a long and detailed rehearsal of "the glorious deeds of the Lord," records the base ingratitude and induration of the people. It is a monument of divine grace and human infidelity. To each series of covenantal acts the poet records the "in spite of all this" of disobedience. God's intent was that they should set their hope on him and keep his commandments, but

> They did not keep God's covenant,
> but refused to walk according to his law.
> They forgot what he had done,
> and the miracles that he had shown them.
>
> Psalm 78:10

So the indictment continues.

Man's history is given him to live responsibly in it. It is not a meaningless chaos of succeeding crises, but the theatre of divine action where issues of transcendent importance are at stake, where the ineradicable imperative of the *"thou shalt"* and *"thou shalt not"* is trumpeted from the battlements of the Most High. Israel was chosen to be God's possession (Pss. 33:12; 78:68; 106:5), but the reiterated theme is constantly marred with the confession, "Both we and our fathers have sinned" (105:6a). The life of worship is rescued from otherworldliness and irresponsible ecstasy by the repeated insistence upon moral obedience. It is significant that the Psalter should

open with a little *mashal* of the two ways, as though it were
designed to remind the Israelite that in worship he is not
delivered from the recognition of what he really is and what
he ought to be, that the truly blessed are the obedient, and
that

The distresses of choice are our chance to be blessed.[2]

That there were many who made worship a mere formality,
a drawing near with their mouths and honoring God with their
lips while their hearts were far from him (Isa. 29:13), was inevitable. The cult is always subject to such corruptions. Festivals become holidays, and fasts, conventional propriety. But
there were liturgies which condemned such behavior and re-
called the ancient obligations:

Is not this the fast that I choose:
　　to loose the bonds of wickedness,
　　to undo the thongs of the yoke,
　to let the oppressed go free,
　　and to break every yoke?
Is it not to share your bread with the hungry,
　　and bring the homeless poor into your house;
　when you see the naked, to cover him,
　　and not to hide yourself from your own flesh?
　　　　　　　　　　　　　　　　Isaiah 58:6-7

We should expect that the covenant would be a central theme
in Israel's worship. At least two liturgies have been preserved
which were used in the annual celebration of the covenant-
renewal festival (Pss. 50, 81), but the appeal to covenant memory and covenant allegiance is not infrequent elsewhere (Pss.
44:17; 74:20; 78:10; 103:18; cf. Pss. 105:8, 10; 89:35). The cult
brings the ancient events into the present, and their present
meaning is that Israel is *now* accountable for her historical
life to the God who has created history and rules over it to
realize his purpose in the creation of the universe. In all these
psalms and in many others, Israel is witnessing to the interior

[2] W. H. Auden, *For the Time Being,* from *The Collected Poetry of W. H. Auden* (New York: Random House, 1945), p. 452.

"historicity" of her existence in the world, or rather, is listening to the witness to the historical nature of her life before God.

God meets each man in the particular history of his own life. This personal history is rooted in that of the community with its historical memories and future hopes. The individual does not stand over against the community, but finds his support and confidence in it. So he is addressed, as in the ancient laws, by the personal "Thou." In the hymns and laments, the power of the divine *pathos* enters into holy relation with the heart of man, and always in the concreteness of the divine activity in relation to human activity.

In Psalm 103, for example, we have a vivid portrayal of man's history as it is related to God's history. It is an intensely personal effusion of the heart of a man. There is no brooding self-centeredness here. The participles record the divine benefits: forgetting, forgiving, healing, redeeming, crowning, satisfying (vss. 1-5). The iniquities, diseases, frailties, sins, and weaknesses of man are comprehended within the stability and steadfastness of God. The fluctuations of the human spirit are understood by one who knows our frame and remembers we are dust (vs. 14). Man's life is fleeting and withers like the flower of the field, but the covenant love of the Holy One is everlasting to the obedient and faithful. His throne is established in the heavens. The soul of man takes flight from all egocentricity and rests in the security of an ultimate and omnipotent goodness, which is more generous than man deserves, yet never surrenders its demands for faithfulness and obedience. It is not without significance that all these ancient rituals are fashioned in the rhythms and patterns of poetry, for poetry is man's best way of saying what is deepest within him. Here again we see that the manner of speaking is for Israel a matter of moment. Israel knows that words must be taken seriously. So our poem ends as it began, "Bless the Lord, O my soul," and all the intervening words are meant to serve the single purpose of motivating the soul's single-minded exultation of praise and adoration.

Like history, the Torah is drawn into the sphere of the divine holiness. It is holy because it is divine speaking. It is holy because God is entering into a live encounter with his people in which they are called to listen. It is holy because in his words

God is telling Israel about his will and purpose, and pointing the direction she should go. It is holy because it was first given in the holy events surrounding the giving of the covenant on the heights of Sinai. Israel is a holy people if she keeps covenant and obeys Torah. The Teaching moves with history, accompanies Israel on her way into the future, and calls her to choice and decision. It is a summons to faithfulness and allegiance. Without it, Israel would be lost in her perplexities as to what she ought to do in the midst of a confused and deeply troubled history. So the cult ministers to her need. The priests and the cultic prophets mediate the demands of the covenant. On the occasion of the covenant-renewal festival, Israel listens to the ancient demands of the Decalogue and the other laws, and in listening becomes contemporary with the fathers who first listened to them. She remembers again the wonders of the past, and the unmotivated grace which prompted them. These are the incentive to obedience. Without them, the Teaching would be lifeless and sterile. But Israel rejoices in the gift of the Torah. It is no burden to be borne with resignation, but a divine vade mecum to direct her on her course through life.

It is an awesome experience to stand before the Temple gates to seek admittance to its holy precincts. The pilgrims come from all over the land to seek the Holy Presence, but before they enter they participate in the liturgy of entrance. The words are reminiscent of early days:

> O Lord, who shall sojourn in thy tent?
> Who shall dwell on thy holy hill?
>
> Psalm 15:1

The cultic personnel give answer:

> He who walks blamelessly and does what is right.
>
> Psalm 15:2a

Then follows the elaboration in concrete terms. He must be a man of utter integrity, who "speaks truth from his heart," who does not slander, does not reproach his neighbor, who despises the reprobate but honors those who reverence God, whose honesty is so thoroughgoing that he will swear even to

his own hurt, who will not put out his money at interest, and
will not take a bribe against the innocent. The man who does
these things will know security, for his way of life is ordered
by the will and purpose of the Lord of man's history. In another little liturgy, the same note is sounded, but with even
greater impressiveness. The choirs sing:

> The earth belongs to Yahweh and all its fullness,
>   the world and they who dwell in it;
> for he has founded it upon the seas,
>   and established it upon the rivers.
>
> Psalm 24:1-2

Again we hear the pilgrim cry, "Who shall stand in his holy
place?" and again the answer comes in much the same vein:

> He who has clean hands and a pure heart,
>   who does not lift up himself to falsity,
>   and does not swear deceitfully.
>
> Psalm 24:4

Such a man will receive the blessing. This is the nature of the
community who "seek the face of Jacob's God." Now the urgency of the great imperatives!

> Lift up your heads, O gates!
>   and be lifted up, O ancient doors!
>   that the King of glory may come in.
>
> Psalm 24:7

Yahweh of hosts is Israel's glorious king. Such hymns are
early, and witness to the influence of the ancient covenant
teachings of Israel. A similar liturgy is preserved in Isaiah
33:14-16; there, too, we discern the same authentic accents. All
of these rituals exhibit a similar way of speaking. We learn
from them what it involves for the worshiper to stand in the
presence of the Holy One, what kind of person may lay hold
on the ultimate resources for life, and what the nature of the
goodness is that is required of him.

Yet there were other demands than those of moral rectitude

that the Israelite believed were asked of him. With the other peoples of the ancient Near East, he shared the conviction that he must not come to the sanctuary empty-handed. Sacrificial offerings were the customary means of drawing near to God, either to receive the benefits of his blessing or to be reconciled with him or to express thanksgiving. Such practices, since they were closely related to similar offerings among the Canaanites, easily opened the way to syncretism. Because they were borrowed, they came to acquire the same associations. Many of the rituals of the Psalter were accompanied by sacrifices, such as those offered before entrance into battle (Ps. 20). These acts easily became ends in themselves. The worshiper believed that the act was sufficient *ex opere operato* to incur the divine favor. Sacrifices of this sort were denounced by the prophets (I Sam. 15:22; Hos. 6:6; Amos 5:22-24; Mic. 6:6-8; Jer. 7:21-23; etc.). The protest registered itself in the cult also. In a liturgy of thanksgiving (Ps. 40:1-12), the devotee rejoices in the glad news of his deliverance and rises to the heights of clear vision as he rejects all burnt offerings and appeals to the law written on the heart (cf. Jer. 31:31-34).

> Sacrifice and offering thou dost not desire;
> but thou hast given me an open ear.
> Burnt offering and sin offering
> thou hast not required.
> Then I said, "Lo, I come;
> in the roll of the book it is written of me;
> I delight to do thy will, O my God;
> thy law is within my heart."

> Psalm 40:6-8

There is an offering greater than all sacrifices that is pleasing to God, the spontaneous outburst of the heart in gratitude and adoration and praise (Pss. 51:15-16; 69:30-33). But the worshiper is not content to rest in the joys of forgiveness or of deliverance. His first impulse is to teach others of the ways of God with men (Ps. 51:13) and to invite the oppressed to see what he has done, that they may be glad, "for the Lord hears the needy, and does not despise his own that are in bonds" (Ps. 69:32-33). In these psalms and others, prayer is separated

from sacrifice. The prayer is itself the sacrifice, "the offering of
the lips," the surrender and dedication of the heart. *Instead of
sacrifice, prayer:* this is the notable advance that was made under prophetic influence in Israel's worship. The prophets have
interiorized religion, and liberated it from the slaughter of
calves and bulls. So the suppliant can appear before Yahweh
with his own words, beseeching him that they may be reckoned
as sacrifice:

> Let my prayer be counted as incense before thee,
>   and the lifting up of my hands as the evening sacrifice.
>   Psalm 141:2

The compensations of obedience are a constant theme of
the psalmists. No rewards are greater than those which come
from doing the will of God. The blessed or happy man is he
whose way is blameless (Ps. 119:1-2). The Torah is his delight
because it teaches him the ways of God, guides him in the
straight paths, gives him life and vitality, inspires him with
hope and trust, sets him free from bondage so that he may walk
at liberty, fortifies and comforts him in grief, endows him with
treasures above gold and silver, sheds light on the way he takes,
and kindles his heart with joy and gladness. It is the greatest
wealth a man can possess. It was good for him to be afflicted
because it taught him the divine statutes (Ps. 119:71). The
thought of the gift of the Teaching stirs him to praise, and in
the house of his pilgrimage its words become songs for his
singing (Ps. 119:54). The long psalm has many moods and
accents, but they are all guided by the divine leading, and
mastered by the divine authority.

The troubled conscience of Israel is brought into the presence of God in the worship of the sanctuary. In the laments
and confessions, we listen to the cries of those who are afflicted
by their sense of guilt. The penitential psalms (Pss. 6, 32, 38,
51, 102, 130, 143), which Martin Luther called Pauline, search
the hidden places of the heart, expose all the sins and frailties
that distract it, and describe the incomparable joys of forgiveness and reconciliation. These penitents betray an amazing
knowledge of their own hearts. They will not deceive themselves, plead extenuating circumstances, minimize their of-

fenses, or revel in excessive introspection. All their griefs and woes and despairs are lifted up to the Holy One who hears. It is moving to see how these psalms seldom end on the self-centered note. They bring into their horizon the afflictions and needs of the whole worshiping community. Psalm 32 opens in the manner of other psalms with the twofold blessing:

> Blessed is he whose transgression is forgiven,
>   whose sin is covered.
> Blessed is the man to whom the Lord imputes no iniquity,
>   and in whose spirit there is no deceit.
>
>   Psalm 32:1-2

So long as he does not declare his sin, his body wastes away, his strength is dried up as by the summer's heat. But then he acknowledges his sin and confesses his transgressions, and receives forgiveness. But he does not rest here. He calls upon everyone who is godly to offer prayer in the time of distress, in the rush of great waters. More than that, he now offers to teach and guide others in the way they should go. So he concludes with the joyous summons:

> Be glad in the Lord, and rejoice, O righteous,
>   and shout for joy, all you upright in heart!
>
>   Psalm 32:11

Originally, of course, these confessions and laments were composed by individuals in the depths of their need. But they became the possession of the community of faith. They have continued to be spoken and heard throughout the course of the history of the Jewish and Christian communities and have there become the native speech of all who know their guilt and seek the solace and release of forgiveness. Not only Augustine and Savonarola and Teresa and John Wesley and Martin Luther but countless others have spoken them as their own most inward thoughts. They are man's ultimate entreaty that he may be what he was created to be:

> Create in me a clean heart, O God,
>   and put a new and right spirit within me.
>
>   Psalm 51:10

Israel has given men words to speak in the presence of the
Holy One. They defy the barriers of time and place and become the interior possession of all who would say what is deepest in the heart to say. They are the authentic outpourings of
the heart and the sure corrective to the bane of sentimentality
and commonplace and triviality.

Surely the prophetic voice is heard in the liturgies. We hear
it in different kinds of liturgical speech. Let us examine several of them. Psalm 12 opens with a lament and a cry for help.
The faithful have vanished from among men; everywhere there
is lying and deceit, flattery and duplicity. Then follows a prayer
that the ungodly may not prevail. Thereupon, the prophet
speaks his word:

> "Because the poor are despoiled, because the needy groan,
>   I will arise," says the Lord;
> "I will place him in the safety for which he longs."
> The promises of the Lord are promises that are pure,
>   silver refined in a furnace on the ground,
>   purified seven times.
>
> Psalm 12:5-6

We need not be told that such oracles belong to the heart
of the old traditions or that the prophet is here perpetuating
them in the manner and with the eloquence characteristic of
him. Psalm 75 opens with a song of thanksgiving recounting
"the wondrous deeds"; then follows the oracle of the prophet
speaking for Yahweh:

> At the set time which I appoint
>   I will judge with equity.
> When the earth totters, and all its inhabitants,
>   it is I who keep steady its pillars.
> I say to the boastful, "Do not boast!"
>   and to the wicked, "Do not lift up your horn."
>
> Psalm 75:2-4

Psalm 81, belonging to the rituals of the covenant-renewal
festival, is a superb example of authentic prophetic speech.
In the heart of it, we listen to the central words of the covenant
faith:

Hear, O my people, while I admonish you!
O Israel, if you would but listen to me!
There shall be no strange god among you;
    you shall not bow down to a foreign god.
I am the Lord your God,
    who brought you up out of the land of Egypt.
Open your mouth wide and I will fill it.

Psalm 81:8-10

Psalm 50 belongs to the same situation; there, too, we experience the activation of the ancient events. Always, Israel is
called to hear the Word, and always it calls her to account,
places her under divine judgment, and summons her to turning and repentance. Moreover, she is always put in the position
where an answer is required of her, at the place of the Yes or
the No. It is her destiny that is at stake.

In the worship of the Temple, the divine rule is celebrated.
We hear Israel's confession, "Yahweh reigns" (or "is King"). No
theme was designed to stir the feelings of Israel more deeply
than this, and nowhere does her enthusiasm and joy rise to
greater heights. It was indeed the central affirmation of the
old covenant faith. When the pilgrims from all over the land
converged upon Jerusalem and the national sanctuary, they
were well aware that they were approaching the place where
Yahweh was present as King in the Holy of Holies, that it was
to him they owed their past history, and that it was to him
they were to look for the future.

It is probable that annually, at the New Year, Yahweh's en-
thronement was celebrated in the Temple. A number of hymns
probably preserve the account of such an event (Pss. 47, 93,
96-99). In Mesopotamia, too, the New Year was celebrated with
liturgies and prayers in connection with the god's enthrone-
ment. Israel's hymns have affinities with these rituals, both in
style and in content—chiefly, perhaps, in the conquest of primeval chaos and in the creation of the earth. But there are
differences, too, for Yahweh's rule extends over the realms of
both nature and history indivisibly. It is significant that the
nations play so important a role in these Israelite hymns. God's
rule extends over all the earth. He conquers the nations. He
is the Judge of all peoples, and he judges with equity and truth

and righteousness, that is, according to the relationship which
he bears to history.

Psalm 47 is in many ways the best exemplar of the enthrone-
ment hymn. It opens on a pitch of great excitement and Oriental realism.

> Clap your hands, all peoples!
> Shout to God with loud songs of joy!
>
> Psalm 47:1

As is characteristic of all the hymns, the motive for this ecstatic
jubilation follows:

> For the Lord, the Most High is terrible,
> a great king over all the earth.
>
> Psalm 47:2

Then the conquest of the nations and the election of Israel
are described. The second strophe (Ps. 47:5-7) is even more
exuberant than the first. God ascends his royal throne to the
sound of great shouting and the blast of the trumpet while
the people grow lyrical in their rejoicing. Again the motive
is given:

> For God is the king of all the earth.
>
> Psalm 47:7a

The final strophe (Ps. 47:8-10) portrays God seated on his
throne, ruling over the nations who have now become one with
the people of the God of Abraham. The Lord of history has
become Lord of all the earth. The promise to Abraham, the
father, has been fulfilled (Gen. 12:1-3), a glorious finale!

The other hymns express the same joy and enthusiasm.
Yahweh has great prestige and honor in the earth. He reigns
in power and majesty over all the world (Ps. 97:9). All the
powers hostile to him have been conquered, and nature joins
with history—the heavens and earth, the sea, and the fields
together with the people of history—to proclaim his sovereignty. But one word more. The King who reigns is a lover
of justice who establishes equity and righteousness in Jacob (Ps.
99:4).

But how is the temporal kingship related to God's dominion? We have seen that there were radical tensions here to which the prophets of Israel bear witness. The earthly king of David's line is the Anointed, the chosen servant, vicegerent, and representative of Yahweh. Upon him the people depend for the stability of the social order. But he is accountable to Yahweh for the character of his rule. If the kingdom is to prosper, he must exemplify the kind of behavior consistent with the covenant relation of the ruling member of the royal line with Yahweh. As king, his power and vitality extend wherever he reigns. His conduct influences the welfare of the social order, his relationships with other nations, and even the productivity of the soil. The vital power in him extends throughout the whole Israelite community. But this mysterious potency is no inherent quality which he possesses. It is dependent upon his righteousness and justice, which are the active relationships that Yahweh bears to his people through him. It is not surprising that a number of royal hymns and liturgies have been preserved, for the king occupies a position of importance in the royal cult, and it is to him that the people look for the prosperity and well-being and peace that he can give as Yahweh's chosen servant.

One of the most impressive of the royal hymns is Psalm 72. It was probably composed for the occasion of the king's accession to the throne, and may well have been employed on many such occasions. It is a superb illustration of the power which words have in the cult. Who the speaker is we are not told, but it could easily have been a prophet. The style is characteristic of the royal court, exaggerated and inflated, yet solemn and measured in its rhythms. The cohortatives follow one upon another in quick succession; the prophet means to include all good wishes for a just and prosperous reign. But more than that, he gives us an insight into what kind of a person the good king should be, the qualities of the just ruler, the activities which will ensure the blessing of the people. He begins *in medias res:*

> Give the king thy justice, O God,
> and thy righteousness to the royal son!
>
> Psalm 72:1

What this means is clearly stated:

> May he judge thy people with righteousness,
>   and the poor with justice.
> May he defend the cause of the poor of the people,
>   give deliverance to the needy,
>   and crush the oppressor.
>
> Psalm 72:2, 4

Petitions of quite another kind are mixed with these: for prosperity, long reign, world-wide dominion, great wealth, and much else. But all these are clearly contingent upon a righteous rule. So the plea that all kings may fall down before him, all nations serve him, is followed significantly with a strophe which gives the basis for the foregoing pleas:

> For he delivers the needy when he calls,
>   the poor and him who has no helper.
> He has pity on the weak and the needy,
>   and saves the lives of the needy.
> From oppression and violence he redeems their life;
>   and precious is their blood in his sight.
>
> Psalm 72:12-14

It is consistent with such portrayals that the king of the royal line of David should be humble. It is scarcely too much to say that humility is the first requirement of a good king. He knows he is but a man and that he has been chosen as Yahweh's representative to rule with those qualities which characterize Yahweh's relation to him and to his people. Justice and righteousness are concretely interpreted in the terms of obligation to all who are in need. Again we hear the categorical imperative: the powerful must use their power for the defense of the weak. The prophetic protests against the mighty and their support of the disinherited have penetrated the sanctuary. It is notable, however, that in the presence of the Holy One Enthroned there is less of outrage and passionate invective and more of persuasion, pleading, and outpouring of the heart. There are those, to be sure, who boast of armaments and security, but he who is the Lord's Anointed Servant can boast only in the name of God (Ps. 20:7; cf. Jer. 9:23-24). A king's prestige and honor (*kabod*) lie in his compassion and justice. He is humble, not only because he knows he is a man, but because he knows he can fulfill his obligations to his people only by dependence upon the source of all justice and righteousness. That is what Psalm 72 and other royal petitions are telling us. *In Israel, the sign of royalty is humility.* The responsibilities of power weigh so heavily upon the king that he must hasten to the sanctuary for help in his weakness.

There are other words we hear in the sanctuary. They are the cries of all who flee there for refuge in time of peril and for help in time of distress. These are the laments. It is noteworthy that they are more numerous than any other literary type, even than the hymns of praise and adoration. The people that rises to the heights of adoration and exultant praise is also the people who travails in the abyss of suffering and pain. For to whom could the afflicted go when there was no helper in the land but to the place where his glory dwelleth? In the Presence of the Invisible One Enthroned, he could hear the holy name spoken, and to him he could address his miseries and fears. The suppliant does not spend his time in vague generalities; rather, he enumerates in concrete and passionate detail all the perplexities of his soul. How urgent he is in his cries, how passionate in his pleadings, how insistent in his imploring for an answer! For he who reigns often hides his face and dwells remote in the darkness.

Yet this is not what is most notable in the laments. It is rather that penetrating nearly all of them there sounds the "nevertheless" of confidence and trust. It is a confidence that the right will yet be vindicated, truth find a Champion, grief and sorrow be turned to joy. It is a joy not so much of material gain and prosperity as of confidence in the assurance granted by him who speaks in his own first person, "I am your God. I will help you. I will deliver and redeem you in your plight." In the sanctuary, the sufferer comes to view his troubles in an ultimate perspective, in the pure light which dispels all the preoccupation with the harassing immediacies of existence (cf. Ps. 73:16 ff.). Let us now turn to the laments themselves that they may bear their own testimony to the "nevertheless" of faith and trust. In Psalm 13, we hear that ancient and characteristic cry of the one in darkness:

How long, O Lord? Wilt thou forget me for ever?
  How long wilt thou hide thy face from me?
How long must I bear pain in my soul,
  and have sorrow in my heart all the day?
How long shall my enemy be exalted over me?

                        Psalm 13:1

Then comes the petition, "Consider and answer me, O Lord,
my God!" But the resolution rings out at the close:

But I have trusted in thy steadfast love;
  My heart shall rejoice in thy salvation.
I will sing to the Lord,
  because he has dealt bountifully with me.

                        Psalm 13:5

At the center of laments such as these, we hear the same words
of interior assurance and trust:

My times are in thy hand.

                        Psalm 31:15a

In God, whose word I praise,
  in God I trust without fear.
What can flesh do to me?

                        Psalm 56:4

I cry to God, Most High,
  to God who fulfills his purpose for me.

                        Psalm 57:2

A superbly spoken plaint is given us in the lament of Psalms
42-43. It is a profoundly poignant expression of longing for
the divine presence. There is not an excessive word in the
whole outcry. Its authenticity is too real and deep for prolixity.
Its images are so rich, its cadences so stirring, its refrains so
passionate that it engages the hearer's participation and invites him to speak it for himself. It is a monument of human
grief and pain. For one thing the suppliant longs above all
others, that he may go to the sanctuary to participate in its
worship: its processions and singing and high festival.

> Deep calls to deep
> at the thunder of thy cataracts;
> all thy waves and billows
> have gone over me.
>
> Psalm 42:7

But always there is the resolution of faith:

> Why art thou cast down, O my soul,
> and why art thou disquieted within me?
> Hope in God, for I shall again praise him,
> my help and my God.
>
> Psalm 42:5; also, Psalms 42:11; 43:5

This is the way of Israel in her worship.

But there is more. The laments disappear and are transmuted into other words which now are all of faith and trust and only little of weeping (Pss. 4, 11, 16, 23, 27, 62, 106, 131). One senses that these men of Israel have found peace and serenity beyond all their sorrows and fears and shames:

> In peace I will lie down and sleep;
> for thou alone, O Lord, makest me dwell in safety.
>
> Psalm 4:8

> Even though I walk in the valley of deep darkness,
> I fear no evil;
> For thou art with me.
>
> Psalm 23:4

We are now prepared to understand why it is "good" for Israel to worship God. It is good because in worship she has discerned the source of her existence and the destiny to which she is called. It is good because her historical life is ordered and steadied by the rule of a transcendent Lord. It is good because in the cult she hears the word of forgiveness. It is good because behind and within her life there is an ultimate love which comprehends all, judges in terrible wrath, and yet is merciful. This is why Israel can praise God even for his judgment upon her. In his judgment, God is manifesting himself as holy, righteous, jealous, and just. In her worship, Israel realizes that she is free from the slaveries which enslave the hearts of men. It would seem that the original deliverance from bondage had conditioned her whole way of thinking and living and speaking. For in the hymns, laments, confessions, thanksgivings, songs of trust, and blessings, we are listening to the words of released and liberated men. In the sanctuary, these men are free to speak, free to pray, free to confess their sins, free to disclose the awful secrets of the heart, free (as the prophets are) to call out in almost blasphemous cries, but also free to sing and praise and adore, and in this last freedom they are free indeed, for they have been delivered from the egocentricities and self-obsessions which lay men low and make them trivial and caviling.

It is not surprising, therefore, that as the Psalter draws to a close the sound of singing grows ever more triumphant and joyous. These men of Israel are praising God that he alone is God and that the gods of the nations are but idols. They are singing because there is One who sits enthroned above the praises of Israel and hears their songs of gratitude (Ps. 22:2). Israel is liberated in her acknowledgment of her relation to a transcendent God, who cannot be fettered by the work of man's hands nor by the sophistries of their thoughts. The true Israel is free in the only freedom available to man. Ever and again she sings the *magnalia Dei,* and she does not weary in rehearsing them. She is deeply stirred by the excitement of the holy hour and the ecstasy of the festivals, by the sound of the trumpet and the loud shouting, and by the great processionals, for she comes before God with the memories of the glorious deeds spoken and activated into the present and with the expectations for the future contemporized in holy rituals and glad celebrations.

> Praise him with trumpet sound;
>   praise him with lute and harp!
> Praise him with timbrel and dance;
>   praise him with strings and pipe!
> Praise him with sounding cymbals;
>   praise him with loud clashing cymbals!
> Let everything that breathes praise the Lord!
> Praise the Lord!
>
> Psalm 150:3-6

6
The Way of the Future

ISRAEL HAS A FUTURE IN THE WORLD. SHE HAS A particular future because she has a particular past. History is deeply lodged within her self-understanding so that the question of its outcome is the constant preoccupation of the sacred writers from very early times. The time appointed her by the grace of God never permits her the security of the present. No present is ever the consummation intended or desired by God. Every present is stamped with the seal of the "not yet." There were those, to be sure, who sought to congeal the present, but against this the vicissitudes of time and the interior dynamic of the historical faith registered its emphatic protest. Over the whole Old Testament there is inscribed the preposition "until," and it is not without significance that its latest book, in a context of august imagery and mythological pageantry, should throb with the anticipation of the demonstration of God's final sovereignty expressed in the "until" of faith (Dan. 4:23-32; 7:1-22). So Israel's existence is always provisional, tentative, and preliminary to what is still to come. What is remarkable is that this note of contingency is struck most firmly at those points where human pride and power assert themselves with greatest daring. Even the Temple and the cult must submit to this tentativeness, for ultimate loyalties were often most subject to corruption and compromise by those who sought to exploit them for their own purposes and interests.

The future is consummated in the coming of God. He who came at the beginning to call a people into history and for history will come in the decisive hour of "the end." The God of Israel is a coming God. He comes as event and in event. He comes and goes, comes and goes, as the patriarchs and the prophets so well knew, sometimes to their perplexity and despair. Life and history are punctuated by these comings;

they are times of revelation, of the divine appearing with words, and the sanctuaries are the monuments to these divine arrivals. The God who comes in the present has come in the past, and in the present he recalls the past; but what is more important is that he points to the future. The coming God will come to consummate his intention in the particular history granted to Israel, and through her to all the world. He comes to bring in his kingdom and to determine Israel's destiny. The future is therefore the center of gravity of Israel's faith; the mainspring of her existence; the source of her vitality, optimism, and hope; the time of the resolution of all the ambiguities and inequities of the past (Isa. 40:9-10); the dawn of a new time.

"*Days are coming when*"—this is one of the most characteristic of the ways in which Israel's expectations are expressed. The beginning was the creation of the first day (Gen. 1:1-3); the end will be the last day. The movement of time from first day to last exacts responsibility from Israel, for "the last day" is the time of accounting. The prophets tell us that the time is near and hastening fast; the imminence of "the Day" is its urgency, momentousness, and fatefulness. Then God will assert his rule over all that he has created, and Israel, already from early times and climactically in the latest period of her history, scans the horizons of the times to anticipate its coming. At least, so it was with those who were her truest representatives.

The way of Israel in the world can never be comprehended in terms of the structures of historical existence. Structures there were, to be sure; no people lives without them. There were, for example, the political, social, and religious institutions of nation and cult. There were, too, the ideological structures by which she sought to discern the flux of historical movement, such as the Deuteronomic attempts to subject it to the neat coherences of moral logic, or the attempts of the priestly historians and the apocalyptic seers to reduce it to the configuration of successive periods. But the attempt of Josiah in the Reformation of 621 B.C. to implement the covenant relation into the political, social, and religious life of the nation ended in failure, and it was precisely its most central affirmations and demands that were the first to be compromised and falsified. Moreover, the attempt to read the meaning of the past in terms of reward for righteousness and punishment for disobedience was in flagrant contradiction to the actual course of Israel's history. Who would venture to say that it is the righteousness of nations that is responsible for their triumphs and prosperity or that it is the pride and sacrilege of nations that explains their defeats and poverty? Surely this is not so in the short ranges of time. There were, of course, profounder renderings of the historical past, as in First and Second Books of Kings, where it is the Word of God that determines the sequence of events and their resolution, above all in the destruction of the state in 587 B.C. But this understanding was achieved in the light of the actual occurrence of the disaster and in the longer ranges of faith as they are seen in retrospect.

Nor can the divine rule of history be simply comprehended in the structures of succeeding periods which the priests and the apocalyptic seers sought to impose upon them. This is to subject the ways of God to human knowledge. But this knowledge is not available to any man. The God of Israel does not yield to such mathematical calculations. Yahweh does not geometrize. The mystery of time is beyond man's knowledge. The ways of the Invisible One Enthroned are not to be subjected to spatial limitations of this kind. There is always a beyondness in the latitudes of God. So he breaks the images which men and empires fashion to symbolize their sovereignty and power, and in their stead he speaks his Word and points to the future (Isa. 41:5-10; 44:9-20, 21-23; 46:1-13; Dan. 2:31-45; 7:19-27).

Here we meet what is in every way one of the central phenomena of the history of the world: the survival of this historical people into the future. Many attempts have been made to give secular or sociological explanations, but none is sufficient to account for the persistence of Israel. If we may venture to give a biblical answer to the question, then we may say that Israel survives because it was God's intention and will that she should survive, not only in the presence of the Christian community which understands itself to be the true Israel, but also in the presence of the faithful Jewish community throughout the world. One may go further and inquire whether she does not survive in order to proclaim God's activity and righteous rule in man's history and in order to remind Christians of the roots and wellsprings of their faith. For when the gospel is heard and Christ is confessed without any recognition of the centuries of preparation or of the streams of faith which converged upon his coming, then the faith becomes but a superficial rendering of what the New Testament is telling us from first page to last.

The orientation of Israel's faith is to the future. The past is prologue to what is yet to come. As we have seen, the epic of the Yahwist moves on from the creation of man to Abraham the father, to the birth of the people, to the reign of David the Lord's Anointed. But the prophets and the leaders of the cult see the promises to Abraham yet to be fulfilled, and they look forward to that denouement when all nations will bless themselves in him and the people of whom he is the progenitor. Similarly, the covenant with David presses on throughout the history of the monarchy and, beyond that, to eschatological time. The prophets are God's watchmen, and they peer into the future to await his coming, with trumpets to their lips. It is God's righteous rule on earth that they proclaim.

The theological basis for Israel's hope and expectation can be stated in various ways. Above all, it is the persistence of the divine purpose in history. The election of Israel was the assertion of that purpose, and to it Yahweh was not recreant. In the covenant, he set his signature to his promise that he will be faithful to his Word, and the love that motivates it is more certain and durable than the foundations of the earth or the stars in their courses (Jer. 31:35-37). In the stability of that assurance, Israel may hope and live. The poets and prophets of Israel employ all the resources of their imaginations to describe the basis of their hopes; the fulfillment of their expectations is guaranteed by what Yahweh is for them. He is the Creator of Israel (Deut. 32:15), and the rock of their sure defense against the perils of historical existence (Deut. 32:4, 15, 18, 30; Isa. 30:29; 44:8; 51-1), the stronghold against the forces which threaten her life (Ps. 71:3; Jer. 16:19), the shield of protection from harm (Pss. 3:3; 47:10; Prov. 3:5), the refuge from the storms that assail her (Pss. 46:1; 71:3; 92:2), the shadow from the torments of heat (Pss. 57:1; 91:1; 121:5), the fountain of living water to assuage the thirst of all who come

(Isa. 55:1-2; Jer. 2:13), the light of Israel (Isa. 10:17; Mic. 6:8; Isa. 60:19-20), the pillar of cloud by day, of fire by night. Yahweh's purpose is very sure, and upon it Israel may depend for her future if she is faithful to that purpose.

A second way in which the basis for Israel's expectations is expressed is that God has a plan for his people and for the world; it is Isaiah of Jerusalem in the midst of a succession of Assyrian aggressions who keeps on stressing the operation of the divine plan in human history (Isa. 5:18-19; 14:24-26; 19:12, 17; 23:8-9; 32:8). Yahweh of hosts is working out his plan, and he will carry it to fulfillment. Jeremiah writes to the discouraged exiles in Babylon, in which he gives them this oracle: "For I know the plans I plan for you, says the Lord, plans for welfare and not for evil, to give you a future and a hope" (Jer. 29:11). He who declares the end from the beginning and before ancient events took place, says, "My counsel shall stand, and I will accomplish all my purpose" (Isa. 46:10). Empires rise and fall, age succeeds age, but in the midst of "all this dark and unintelligible world" the divine purpose is at work, and "the time will come, when" it will be revealed for every eye to behold (Isa. 40:1-11). So the true Israel lives by memories of what God has done; for his remembered deeds are, sometimes darkly and hiddenly, sometimes more manifestly, the harbingers of the future.

In the celebrations of the cult, Israel witnesses to the reality of God's purpose. History is the "drama" of former events and latter events in which God is fulfilling his intention (Isa. 40-55). It is a warfare between the forces of good and the forces of evil, and in this conflict man is forever engaged. The consequences of his choices and actions are fateful, for upon them depend his peace and well-being, his rest, his destiny. What God does for man is good, even in his terrible judgments. He engages ceaselessly in the conflict on the side of the right, and he will have the victory.

The divine purpose in history is also affirmed in the motif of promise and assurance. Man is directed to the future by the assurances of God. The course of events in the great epics is guided by the words vouchsafed to the patriarchs, and the psalmists are sustained and comforted by the words of trust and hope spoken in the assurances of priest and prophet. In the prophets we are constantly listening to the pledge or oath of God that he will act decisively in the future, that his honor may be vindicated among the nations. He will act in order that his ways may be vindicated. He acts *for his own sake,* for his prestige and name in the world (Ezek. 20:44; 36:21-22; 39:7). Further, the words of the prophets are sure to find fulfillment. They will not disappear into thin air, but will be realized in the events to which they point. In all these ways the historical life of men and of nations is undergirded by the assurance that the course of history is not meaningless. Man is called to a divine destiny, and because Israel knows this as no other people, she is the people of destiny.

But this destiny is by no means inevitable so that willy-nilly it will be automatically realized. Nothing could be farther from the divine intention. There were, indeed, those who interpreted it in this way, so that even the covenant assurances were claimed as a ground of security without any recognition of the contingencies which lay at their center. That God's mercy went beyond the demands for obedience is surely true, but man's accountability before the bar of an ultimate justice is never dissolved. Again, history did not reveal the righteous rule of God, either in the lives of individuals or in the careers of nations, in the manner of a simple moral logic or in the immediacy of the present hour. The divine sovereignty is often obscure and mysterious, hidden from human view and clouded from man's sight. Nevertheless, Israel is called to respond to the divine leading. "Surely there is a future, and your hope will not be cut off," says the ancient sage (Prov. 23:18), and in saying so he is but echoing the more dynamic faith of the prophets (cf. Jer. 29:11).

For this future, faithful Israel lives in hope and patient waiting. Since it is from Yahweh, whose very Name is the ground of hope and assurance, that her expectations come, she lives in the confidence that he will vindicate right and requite evil, champion the faithful and defeat the rebellious. Yahweh is the Hope of Israel, even though his absence often afflicts the distraught and anxious heart:

O thou hope of Israel,
    its savior in time of trouble,

why shouldst thou be like a stranger in the land,
like a wayfarer who turns aside to tarry for a night?

Jeremiah 14:8

Among the other ancient Near Eastern religions there was no firm basis for hope in the future. The vitalities of nature could never inspire its devotees with the dynamic which a faith in one God who reveals himself in the events of history kindled in the hearts of the called, chosen, and consecrated people. From the beginning, Israel is summoned to the future of God's finale. Therefore she lives by waiting, even when all the avenues to the future seem closed, as in the prophet Isaiah's time of darkness: "I will wait for the Lord, who is hiding his face from the house of Israel, and I will hope in him" (Isa. 8:16). When history itself seemed to give the lie to Israel's faith in historical revelation and in her uniqueness as the historical people, the exiles could cry out bitterly, "My way is hid from the Lord, and my right is disregarded by my God" (Isa. 40:27 cd). But the prophet could respond in the incomparable lines of victorious assurance, culminating in the call to waiting and trust and faithful walking:

But they who wait for the Lord shall renew their strength,
    they shall mount up with wings as eagles,
they shall run and not be weary,
    they shall walk and not faint.

Isaiah 40:31

Words of expectation are heard again in the courts of the sanctuary. They are spoken by the sufferers who wait for the morning of a just redemption (Pss. 33:20; 27:15; 37:34; 62:1; 130; cf. Lam. 3:19, 23). Utterances such as these win their authenticity from at least two considerations. They are centered in the presence of God and in his sustaining help, and they stand in striking contrast to the false expectations of man generally: in armaments and power (Ps. 20:7; Isa. 30:16; 31:1), in riches (Pss. 49:5-9; 52:7; Job 21:24-28), in princes and potentates (Isa. 7:9; Hos. 4:8; Ps. 146:3), or even in the Temple (Jer. 7:1-15).

The expectations of Israel for the future find their more

ample and spacious expression in the anticipations of the new age. Here we find ourselves on the highway of the great tradition. History is the arena of the ever-emerging new. The uniqueness of events and "times" is such that they cannot be catalogued and classified; at least, what is important in them is new and unrepeatable. They cannot be reduced to stereotypes or be coerced into the patterns of nature. So in the course of Israel's faith we are constantly brought into encounter with new events and new words. They have never happened before and will never happen again. But the prophets of Israel look forward to the future of the new age, the decisively and radically new, a new kind of newness, because it is the consummation and fulfillment of God's purpose in election and the resolution of the ambiguities and inequities of the intervening past by an act of grace. It is important to see that the New Testament, where the consciousness of the newness of the Messianic age is so central, is dependent upon the Old Testament for its categories of newness, and this is only natural, for the anticipation of "the age to come" and all that accompanies it is so marked a feature of Israelite thinking, even though the expression itself is later than the Old Testament.

The new age is of course understood in relation to the old, to all the *magnalia* from the creation to David the king. In many contexts, the sacred writers seem to be thinking of a return or repetition of that seminal period of Israel's faith, the Mosaic age. But it is much more than return or repetition. It is magnified, deepened, and more glorious. It is the consummation of what Yahweh had intended in the initiation of his activity in history. His purpose is now brought to fulfillment. The corruptions and distortions and failures of intervening history, the history of disobedience and infidelity, are overcome by Yahweh's new, eschatological activity. The descriptions of the new age are often drawn from the world of mythological imagery. They are thereby given an amplitude and universality, a cosmic setting and dimension, which, though not absent from the old, are more pronounced and articulate. The new age is introduced in the theater of world history.

As he came in the time of the Exodus, so now God comes to deliver his people from the bondage of Exile (Isa. 48:20; 52:3, 9-10; Jer. 31:11; Mic. 4:10). As he rescued them at the Sea of

Reeds, so he will rescue them on the more spacious stage of world history (Isa. 11:15f.; 43:16ff.; 51:9-10; Zech. 10:10-11), and the nations will see his mighty works and be ashamed of all their might (Mic. 7:15-16). The great deed is sung in hymns of exulting praise as Miriam sang of God's victory on the other side of the waters (Isa. 42:10 ff.; 44:23). The return of Israel to the homeland from all the lands of her Exile is like the sojourn in the desert, but now waters burst forth everywhere (Isa. 41:18; 43:19; 49:8-10). The new Exodus is the time of salvation. Its universality is now proclaimed with great ardor and joy. All the ends of the earth will see the salvation of Israel's God (Isa. 52:7), and they are summoned to turn to him and be saved (Isa. 45:22-23). In Second Isaiah, monotheism is never defined theoretically or abstractly but is the assertion of Yahweh's universal reign over all the nations when they confess him as King and Redeemer. The nations participate in the Exodus event. But more than that, the new time of the new Exodus will see the fulfillment of the predictions of the prophets. Thus the uncertainty of past history is dispelled by the certainty of the new age.

There is a deeper dimension in the prophetic understanding of the new Exodus. It is the time of the divine forgiveness, the liberation from the slavery and bondage of sin. The new age opens with this deed of free grace; the deed is prologue to all the *magnalia* which follow, and it is the true basis for the new redemption (Isa. 44:21-22; 54:7-10). Again the joyous hymns break forth:

> Sing, O heavens, for the Lord has done it;
>   shout, O depths of the earth;
> break forth into singing, O mountains,
>   O forest, and every tree in it!
> For the Lord has redeemed Jacob,
>   and will be glorified in Israel.
>
> Isaiah 44:23

The new event is celebrated with such ecstatic joy because Israel knows that it is unmerited, that it is an act of pure grace. Her new life is lived from the time of forgiveness. The new Israel is the forgiven people. Jeremiah articulates in a word all that lay behind the wonders of this new age, why it was that the people who survived found grace in the desert:

> I have loved you with an everlasting love;
> therefore I have continued my faithfulness to you.
>
> Jeremiah 31:3

In the new age, Yahweh enters into a new relation with his people. One would not have suspected that this would be possible, for the prophets had repeatedly declared that he had rejected them. Thus, Isaiah pronounces the awful verdict: "Thou hast rejected thy people, the house of Jacob" (Isa. 2:6), and other prophets confirm the decision. But then God speaks his "nevertheless," and grants his people the radically new possibility by making them his own again in a new way. From the decision "Not my people," he now turns to his, "You are my people" (Hos. 2:23), and we keep on hearing in many different kinds of contexts the solemn words of covenantal assurance:

> And you shall be my people,
> and I will be your God.
>
> Jeremiah 30:22; cf. Jeremiah 31:1,
> 33; 32:38; Ezekiel 36:28;
> 37:23; Zechariah 8:8; 13:9

We hear the ancient covenant words spoken again, but they are spoken for the time of fulfillment. The sons of Israel will be called the Holy People, the Redeemed of the Lord (Isa. 62:12; cf. Exod. 19:5), the sons of the living God (Hos. 2:1), "the priests of the Lord" and the ministers of God (Isa. 61:6).

The prophets do not leave us in any doubt about the nature of the new bond. Israel will be given a new heart and a new spirit, that is, a new will and disposition and a new motivation, so that she will not only be inclined to the way of obedience, but will desire to do what she ought to do and live and act in the freedom of a new commitment. Yahweh will sprinkle her with clean water that she may be cleansed from her uncleanness; Yahweh will give her again the gift of the land, now transformed and renewed, that she may dwell in it in the way that he intended her to do in the age of Moses:

> For I will take you from the nations, and gather you from all the countries, and bring you into your own land. I will sprinkle clean water upon you, and you shall be clean from all your uncleanness, and from all your idols I will cleanse you. A new heart I will give you, and a new spirit I will put within you; and I will take out of your flesh the heart of stone and give you a heart of flesh. And I will put my spirit within you, and cause you to walk in my statutes and you shall be careful to observe my ordinances. You shall dwell in the land which I gave to your fathers; and you shall be my people, and I will be your God.
>
> Ezekiel 36:24-28

God will be the good Shepherd to lead his people home from their wandering, and there will be one Flock, one Shepherd (Jer. 31:10; Ezek. 34:13 ff.) . Elsewhere the transformation of Israel is described as the new circumcision, not of the flesh, but of the heart, or mind (Deut. 30:6; Jer. 4:4; cf. 9:25-26) . The center about which most if not all of these promises gravitate is the new covenant, which is not subject to the corruptions of time and event but is an eternal covenant of peace (Jer. 32:40; Ezek. 16:60 ff.; Isa. 54:8 ff.; Mal. 3:1; cf. Gen. 9:8-17) .

In an age when the foundations of Judah's national life are destroyed, Jeremiah becomes the radical critic of all the institutional supports by which the community seeks to secure itself, not least among them the Temple when it is used as a place of holy protection (Jer. 7:1-15) . He sees the old age passing away and looks forward to the age of the new covenant, which has its foundation in the wonder of forgiveness:

> Behold, the days are coming, says the Lord, when I will make a new covenant with the house of Israel and the house of Judah, not like the covenant which I made with their fathers when I took them by the hand to bring them out of the land of Egypt, my covenant which they broke, though I was their husband, says the Lord. But this is the covenant which I will make with the house of Israel after those days, says the Lord: I will put my law within them, and I will write it upon their hearts; and I will be their God, and they shall be my people. And no longer shall each man teach his neighbor and each his brother, saying, "Know the Lord," for they shall all know me, from the least of them to the greatest, says the Lord, for I will forgive their iniquity, and I will remember their sin no more.
>
> Jeremiah 31:31-34

The words were remembered, and became the source more
than any other for the faith of the early Christian community
that the new covenant had been realized in Christ (II Cor. 3:4
ff.; Heb. 8:6-13; 10:15-18).

It is essential that we understand all these texts in the total
framework of which they are an integral part. In all of them we
witness the activity of the Word of God yielding fruition. The
Word spoken in the time of election finds its realization in
the fulfillment of the new age. The Word spoken at Sinai is
heard again in the end-time. God speaks his Word, and so great
is its power and vitality that it will accomplish that which he
has always purposed (Isa. 55:10-11). The age of Moses is not a
static reality, an age past and gone and confined to antiquity.
It is present throughout the course of Israel's life. In her worship, Israel is constantly witnessing to its present reality. Yet it
is consummated in the age of fulfillment, for Israel's history
has been one of infidelity and disobedience. The two primary
bases of Israel's faith, election and covenant, continue as the
bases for the great finale of a new redemption and a new covenant. All history is determined by the efficacy of the divine
Word, bodied forth, sometimes in the oracles of the prophets,
sometimes in the liturgies and hymns, sometimes in the his-
tories. Israel has a destiny because the Word of God is addressed
to her in history. This is the ground of her hope and expectation.

Among the memories and expectations associated with the
age of Moses there was one which was destined to assume a role
of great importance, the return of Moses, the mediator of the
covenant and the Torah. Like all the promises associated with
the fulfillment of the assurances in election and covenant, they
are spoken in the first person:

> I will raise up for them a prophet like you from among
> their brethren; and I will put my words in his mouth, and he
> shall speak to them all that I command them.
>   Deuteronomy 18:18

Is this a reference to the covenant mediators, like Joshua,
Samuel, Hosea, and Jeremiah, or is it meant eschatologically?
Certainly it came to be understood in the latter sense, and the
covenanters at Qumran, to whom we owe the Dead Sea Scrolls,
and the early Christians took it in this way. But associated with
the hopes for a Moses redivivus there were others which cen-

tered about the ruler of the royal house of David. As men
looked forward to the coming of Moses as mediator of covenant
and Torah, so they looked forward to the time when David or a
king of David's house would come to inaugurate the reign of
Yahweh's righteous vicegerent. While many of the passages
which describe the king came to be interpreted Messianically,
they were in the first instance directed to Yahweh's representative upon the temporal throne (Isa. 9:1-6; 11:1-8; 32:1 ff.; Mic.
5:2-4; cf. Jer. 30:9; 33:14-18; Ezek. 34:23 ff.; 37:24-28; etc.).
Mosaic and Davidic theology have much in common. Both are
fundamentally directed to the establishment of God's righteous
rule on earth. Both are related to the covenant. Both bear witness to the demands of obedience and faithfulness, despite differences in the apprehension of the relation of law and grace.
It is not difficult to understand, therefore, why, especially in
later writers, the two areas of expectation should sometimes
coalesce.

From very early times the kingship is related to the future.
Already during the United Monarchy, blessings and oracles,
ostensibly emanating from ancient times, were composed in
which David's reign is foretold. Although these compositions
probably come from the time of David, he is nevertheless placed
in the context of ancient anticipation and hope. They are
vaticinia post eventum, prophecies after the event. So in the
Blessing of Jacob (Gen. 49), the aged patriarch, gifted with the
divinatory powers of those approaching death, speaks of the
time when

> The sceptre shall not depart from Judah,
>   nor the ruler's staff from between his feet,
> until he comes to whom it belongs;
>   and to him shall be the obedience of the peoples.
>
> Genesis 49:10

It is probable that David is meant here. Similarly, in the Oracles
of Balaam, the seer speaks in the mysterious and adumbrated
language of vision:

> I see him, but not now;
> I behold him, but not nigh:

> a star shall come forth from Jacob,
> and a scepter shall rise out of Israel.
>
> Numbers 24:17

But the *locus classicus* of all future expectations associated with David is the account of the divine promise to the king (II Sam. 7). As the chosen and anointed servant of Yahweh, David is given the assurance that his kingdom will be made sure before God and that his throne will be established forever (II Sam. 7:16). In the last words of David (II Sam. 23:1-7), the king utters an impressive oracle in which he speaks of the everlasting covenant, "ordered in all things and secure," which God has made with his house, and the ethical note, so characteristic of the royal ideology, is struck:

> When one rules justly over men
>   ruling in the fear of God,
> he dawns on them like the morning light,
>   like the sun shining forth on a cloudless morning,
> like the rain that makes grass to sprout from the earth.
>
> II Samuel 23:4

These ancient royal blessings and visions influenced the prophets and psalmists of Israel. They are enriched and heightened by mythological motifs and images drawn from the rituals of the Canaanites as we find them in the texts from Ugarit, but they are transformed by the context of Messianic expectations centering in the royal line of David's house. The myth serves its purpose by giving to the prophetic oracles a cosmic spaciousness and universality, which was already part of the royal ideology of David's court. The prophet Isaiah, whose expectations are drawn from this court speech rather than from the *magnalia* of the Mosaic age, describes in several elevated utterances the character of the scion of David (Isa. 9:2-7; 11:1-9; 32:1 ff.). A child will be born who will bear regnal names of great portent, upon his shoulders will rest the royal regalia, the age of war will come to an end, all the paraphernalia of battle will be burned, and an age of everlasting peace will ensue. He will sit on David's throne and rule over his kingdom to establish it "with justice and with righteousness, from this time forth and for evermore" (Isa. 9:7). Nature will be so changed that

the wild animals will lie down with the tame, and a little child
will lead them:

> They shall not hurt or destroy
>   in all my holy mountain;
> for the earth shall be full of the knowledge of the Lord
>   as the waters cover the sea.
>
> Isaiah 11:9

History, too, is completely transformed, for the military might
and power of the king, his desire for foreign conquest, and his
vindictiveness all yield to the one end so passionately longed
for, the time of peace. There is no hurt in this age, no venge-
ance or hatred, no arrogance or gloating.

The later prophets continue to stress the moral foundations
of the future king of David's line. The kingdom is always established on the foundations of righteousness and justice. The
king will deal wisely, and his throne name will be "Yahweh
our righteousness" (Jer. 23:5-6). He will shepherd his flock,
and it will live in obedience to the divine requirements, and so
live in security (Ezek. 34:24). Again the king's humility pene-
trates the oracles, and it is worthy of note that it appears in the
context of popular rejoicing:

> Rejoice greatly, O daughter of Zion!
>   Shout aloud, O daughter of Jerusalem!
> Lo, your king comes to you;
>   triumphant and victorious is he,
> humble and riding on an ass,
>   on a colt, the foal of an ass.
>
> Zechariah 9:9

The new age confronts us with the paradox of the lowly king.

The royal liturgies and hymns take up the theme of the prophetic oracles of the future of the Lord's Anointed. David's
throne is secure in the steadfast love and faithfulness of God.
The king is accountable for maintaining the order of his realm
by obedience and covenant faithfulness. But the disobedience
of a king will not alter the divine oath to David that his kingdom will endure as long as the sun and the moon. Not only
David is chosen but Zion also. It is there that Yahweh desires to

dwell in order that he may make a horn to sprout for David and prepare a lamp for his Anointed, but what is more, that he may satisfy the poor with bread. Thus, the hopes of Israel for the future are motivated and grounded in the ultimate assurance that the kingdom of God will come on earth, that her destiny is secure in his promise, and that the future will see the realization of the divine righteousness and justice among men (Ps. 89).

The new age is the age of the Spirit. The gift of the Spirit is a central feature of the coming age. Yahweh will pour out his Spirit to effect a radical change in both nature and history, which exist in sympathetic rapport with each other. The new time is marked by God's "until":

until the Spirit is poured upon us from on high,
    and the wilderness becomes a fruitful field,
and the fruitful field is deemed a forest.
Then justice will dwell in the wilderness,
    and righteousness abide in the fruitful field.
And the effect of righteousness will be peace,
    and the result of righteousness, quietness and trust for ever.
                                                    Isaiah 32:15-17

In eschatological time, Yahweh will pour out his Spirit upon all the people of Israel (Isa. 44:3) and will inspire their sons and daughters with the gift of prophecy (Joel 2:28-29). So the fervent wish of Moses that all the people were prophets will be fulfilled (Num. 11:29). The Spirit rests upon the future king and manifests its presence by equipping him with those qualities which an ideally good king should possess and by endowing him with the power to perform the acts which belong to God's representative on earth:

With righteousness he shall judge the poor,
    and decide with equity for the meek of the earth; . . .
Righteousness shall be the girdle of his waist,
    and faithfulness the girdle of his loins.
                                                    Isaiah 11:4a, 5

Israel's future rests upon the coming of the Spirit. It is the gift for the new age. Its outward and inward events are possible because of it. So the Israel of the future lives according to the Spirit. Its chief marks are power to effect God's will and to act, vitality to live life to the full, inspiration to prophesy, and the desire to be obedient and faithful. When Israel is given the assurance, borrowed from the imagery of neighboring religions, "I will not hide my face from you," this is understood, interestingly, as the presence of the Spirit (Ezek. 39:29). In the Vision of the Valley of Dry Bones, the dead nation is brought to life by its power: "I will put my Spirit within you and you shall live" (Ezek. 37:14). The Magna Charta of freedom transcending all the power of ecclesiastical and political institutions is expressed in the words of the angel to Zerubbabel, the head of the Jewish state: "Not by might, nor by power, but by my Spirit, says the Lord" (Zech. 4:6).

The ways of Israel's past converge in the theology of Second Isaiah. In the heavenly assembly, the prophet hears himself addressed with the call to prepare the way of the Lord, to make straight in the desert a highway for God (Isa. 40:3). This is what the prophet is doing throughout his poems. There were many ways Israel had taken in her course through history, and of these the prophet takes account in his blazing of the highway to the future. The prophets themselves with their predictions and oracles of judgment, the historians with their narration of the traditions of the election-covenant past, the ministrants of the cult with their hymns and liturgies, the teachers of the Torah with the light of its revelation, and the priests with their creation traditions all make their contributions to the drama of the new age. More particularly, the theology of the Mosaic age and of the Davidic royal dynasty coalesce to construct the highway for the coming of God into human history.

In a word, Second Isaiah is composing an eschatalogical drama, albeit in Semitic manner, style, and imagery. Beginning and end form the two foci of his theology. He therefore employs the categories of the ancient myths for the delineation of his protology and eschatology. Beginning is the necessary correlate of end, creation the essential presupposition of consummation. The world of nature participates in the world of God's given time of the coming age, and nature rejoices in acknowledging that she is but the servant of the divine purpose in history. The memories of "the former things" are seminal for the future because at their center lies God's intention for history; they provide the matrix for the expectations to be realized in "the latter things." Thus the constancy of God's purpose stands fast. Throughout the poems the figure of the Servant of the Lord plays a role of central importance, for it is he who stands at the time of the finale to execute his predestined mission as the chosen agent of God's will and purpose. The power and vitality of the Spirit is given him that he may be equipped to perform his appointed task, quietly and courageously and without any show of ostentation. Whether we think of him as the community of Israel or as an individual, he represents the true Israel, the called and chosen servant.

What, then, is this call to which Israel is called, this mission upon which she is sent? First of all and obviously, as the Servant of the Lord, Israel is commissioned to a great service. She is the called and consecrated slave of God, appointed to perform those tasks which belonged to her servitude to him. She is God's burden-bearer laden with the heavy responsibility of the chosen. She must assume those obligations that belong to her vocation as Servant and Elect One, to labor without wearying and complaint, and not to seek any reward save that which God has in store. As Servant, she is called to do her Master's bidding, to be intent upon his Word, and to find in it sufficiency for her life.

But the service of the Servant is more than this. It is also worship, for worship is service (*abodhah*). It is giving thanks to the Creator, looking to him in times of darkness and distress, singing hymns of adoration, and joining in the holy rituals. It is faithfulness to creation, both the creation of the people and the creation of the universe. So the service of the Servant is much more than servility. The mission of the Servant is an august one, in deepest humiliation he towers above all. The relation between Lord and Servant is that of the I and the Thou, the intimate converse between the speaking I and the hearing Thou. The Servant is the forgiven one (Isa. 44:22), and this is the source of the Servant's freedom. It is freedom from fear and anxiety and dread. This is the meaning of the frequent admonition, "Fear not!" It is freedom to an ultimate sovereignty: "I am your King."

It is the mission of Israel to be what she was called and destined by God to be. This is why she is summoned to look to her progenitors, Abraham and Sarah (Isa. 41:8-10; 51:1-3). Israel must look to her heritage, to the sources of her life in history, for in them is already inscribed the interior meaning of her life. As Abraham was called and chosen, so she is called and chosen. As his life was ordered by God, so hers must be. He who blessed Abraham and made him many is still the ground of hope and expectation for the future. The way of Abraham must be Israel's way (cf. Rom. 4). This is the way of help and deliverance, the way for those who seek God, the way which leads to gladness and thanksgiving (Isa. 51:1-3). The way which began with the progenitor is the way of his sons. Such longitudinal ranges are unique in Near Eastern antiquity and in the history of religions. Israel is called to vast perspectives.

It is the mission of Israel to be the agent of God's purpose. She is to identify herself with that purpose and make it her own. To it she is to devote all her energies, even when daunted and discouraged, despised, abhorred by the nations, and the servant of rulers (Isa. 49:5-7). She must press on to the goal of all her striving, the denouement of God's plan, until his kingdom comes, until the nations own his sway and give him the allegiance that is his due. Israel's responsibility to history and to historical destiny is supported by the assurance that the divine purpose will stand, that the divine Word will be confirmed, that the age of felicity will come in which her way will be vindicated by the confessions of the peoples.

It is further the mission of Israel to be the covenant people, but with this there is the corollary that she must also bring other peoples under the reign of the Lord of history, to be one with them in covenant bond, though her special prerogatives as the chosen people are not forfeited. Particularism and universalism are not antithetical but correlative, for Israel's mission is to be the light to the nations, to open the eyes that are blind, and to liberate from prison those that are bound, that God's salvation may reach to the end of the earth (Isa. 42:6-7; 49:6). The foreigner will write on his hand "Belonging to Yahweh," and surname himself by Israel's God (Isa. 44:5), and the nations will come confessing, "God is with you only, and there is no other" (Isa. 45:14d). So God calls out urgently for the conversion of the nations:

Turn to me and be saved,
all the ends of the earth!
For I am God, and there is no other.
By myself I have sworn,
from my mouth has gone forth in righteousness
a word that shall not return:
"To me every knee shall bow,
every tongue shall swear."

Isaiah 45:22-25

The prophet Malachi, a man of quite a different temper and theological outlook from Second Isaiah, also stresses the uniqueness of Israel and its world-wide mission; nowhere, indeed, is the theme of universalism pressed quite so far as with him:

For from the rising of the sun to its setting my name is great among the nations, and in every place incense is offered to my name, and a pure offering; for my name is great among the nations, says the Lord of hosts.

Malachi 1:11

The election of Israel is not a mark of exclusivism and national pride but of responsibility to the nations. She is her truest self, most faithful to her heritage of election and covenant, when she issues the universal invitation, "Ho, every one who thirsts, come to the waters" (Isa. 55:1a).

Further, it is the mission of Israel to lead the nations of the world to peace. It is the most constant as it is the most intense of all her hopes for the future. For a thousand years and more, the little land had been the theater of bloody combat, and again and again Israel had been caught in the vortex of the conflicts between the great empires. So when the prophets picture the ideal age of felicity that is to come, their first thoughts are of peace, which include prosperity and personal well-being, to be sure, but also freedom from foreign aggression. In that age men will lay down their arms; the instruments of war will be destroyed, and men will enjoy the comforts of home and the joys of family life without fear and dread. The king of the future will usher in the age of peace, chariot and battle-bow will be cut off from the land, and

> he shall command peace to the nations;
>   his dominion will be from sea to sea,
>   and from the River to the ends of the earth.
>
> Zechariah 9:10

Israel can summon the nations to peace, for she knows that the resources of peace lie with him who is her peace and whose will is peace for all the nations.

Consistent with the foregoing is the mission of Israel to be the witness of God. Her commission is succinctly stated in the characteristic way of the divine speaking: first, the direct address, "You are my witnesses," and then the divine self-asseveration, "I, I am Yahweh, and besides me there is no savior" (Isa. 43:10-11; cf. vss. 12c, 13). Israel must witness that Yahweh alone is God. The nations of the world gather together to listen to her testimony. None of them of course has such a word as this. They have no such witnesses to speak such words, they know nothing of "the former things," they cannot speak to history because they look to the world of space, to the idols they fashion so meticulously with their hands for strength and support in times of crisis (Isa. 41:7; 44:9-20). Israel's witness is to the singleness of the Lord who determines the destinies of men and of nations (Isa. 43:8-13).

It is the mission of the Servant of the Lord to be present at the time of reckoning and accounting, and at that time to perform his supreme work for the nations of the world. The mission of the Servant is fulfilled in his sufferings and death. He offers himself voluntarily as a sacrifice without blemish, the ultimate and sufficient offering for sin and transgression, takes upon himself the sins and crimes of which the nations and their rulers are guilty, and substitutes himself for them as the final verdict is to be pronounced. In the confessional lament of Isaiah 53:1-9, we listen to the nations speaking as they describe the suffering and rejection and abandonment of the Servant, all his pains and griefs and sorrows:

> He was despised and rejected by men;
>   a man of sorrows and acquainted with grief;
> as one from whom men hide their faces
>   he was despised and we esteemed him not. . . .

But he was wounded for our transgressions,
   he was bruised for our iniquities;
upon him was the chastisement that made us whole,
   and with his stripes we are healed.

Isaiah 53:3, 5

The lines must be read in the context of the whole of the eschatological drama, from beginning to end, from creation to redemption, from the beginnings of historical revelation to its culmination, from Abraham to the Servant. In the final hour of awareness, the nations come to realize that the Servant is bearing their griefs and carrying their sorrows, but, beyond that, that God is working out his purpose through him, that it is his purpose that the Servant should suffer and die for them, and that it is through the suffering and death of the Servant that they are to be healed and made whole. The hour of deepest humiliation and degradation and rejection is the hour when the Servant rises to his highest elevation as the commissioned instrument of God. The words were meant for the future, but for the future made present by faith. In the passion and death of Jesus, the Christian community confesses that in him the words were fulfilled, and in so doing it confesses that the whole meaning of Israel from its earliest beginnings finds in him its ultimate revelation. And with the opening words of the prophecy (Isa. 52:13), it confesses, too, that God has greatly exalted his Servant.

Finally, it is the mission of Israel to call the world to rejoicing:

Sing, O barren one, who did not bear;
   break forth into singing and cry aloud,
   you who have not been in travail!

Isaiah 54:1

Again and again, and from her beginnings, Israel is summoned to gladness and thanksgiving. In eschatological time even the forces of nature loose their ancient fetters that they may break forth into song. The universe is stirred to ultimate joy, but this ultimate joy is understood against the background of the travailings of history and in the faith of God's overcoming of all earth's rebellions and infidelities and griefs in mighty victory. As creation always aroused the poets of Israel to adoration and praise, so now in the time of God's accomplishment of his purpose in history and creation the whole creation sings:

> Sing, O heavens, for the Lord has done it;
>> shout, O depths of the earth;
> break forth into singing, O mountains,
>> O forest, and every tree in it!
> For the Lord has redeemed Jacob,
>> and will be glorified in Israel.
>
> Isaiah 44:23

The call to the prophet summoned him to prepare the way of the Lord, and this, at the deepest levels of her life in the world, is the mission of Israel. It is the way of Israel to make straight a highway for her God.

A Selected Bibliography

Anderson, Bernhard, *Understanding the Old Testament,* Englewood Cliffs, New Jersey, 1957.

Alt, Albrecht, *Die Urspruenge des israelitischen Rechts,* Kleine Schriften zur Geschichte des Volkes Israel, Erster Band, pp. 278-332, Munich, 1953.

Balscheit, B. and Eichrodt, W., *Die soziale Botschaft des Alten Testaments fuer die Gegenwart,* Basel, n.d.

Boman, Thorlief, *Hebrew Thought Compared with the Greek.* Library of History and Doctrine, Philadelphia, 1960.

Buber, Martin, *The Prophetic Faith,* New York, 1949.

Bultmann, Rudolph, *Primitive Christianity in Its Contemporary Setting,* translated from the German by R. H. Fuller, New York, 1956.

Childs, Brevard, *Myth and Reality in the Old Testament,* Studies in Biblical Theology, No. 27, London, 1960.

Bible Key Words, from R. Kittel's *Theologisches Woerterbuch zum Neuen Testament,* translated and edited by J. R. Coates, Vol. I, New York, 1951; Vol. II, New Work, 1958.

Dahl, N. A., *Das Volk Gottes: eine Untersuchung zum Kirchenbewusstsein des Urchristentums,* Oslo, 1941.

Dodd, C. H., *The Bible To-day,* New York, 1947.

Eichrodt, Walther, *Man in the Old Testament,* Studies in Biblical Theology No. 4, translated from the German by K. and R. Gregor Smith, Chicago, 1951.

———, *Israel in der Weissagung des Alten Testaments,* Zurich, 1951.

Fichtner, J., *Die altorientalische Weisheit in ihrer israelitischen-juedischen Auspraegung,* Giessen, 1933.

Gottwald, Norman K., *A Light to the Nations: an Introduction to the Old Testament,* New York, 1959.

Hempel, Johannes, *Das Ethos des Alten Testaments,* Berlin, 1938.

Herberg, Will, *Judaism and Modern Man: an Interpretation of Jewish Religion,* New York, 1951.

Heschel, A. J., *God in Search of Man,* Philadelphia, 1956.

———, *The Sabbath,* New York, 1951.

Jacob, Edmond, *Theology of the Old Testament,* translated from the French by Arthur W. Heathcote and Philip J. Allcock, New York, 1958.

Johnson, A. R., *The One and the Many in the Israelite Conception of God,* Cardiff, 1942.

———, *The Vitality of the Individual in the Thought of Ancient Israel,* Cardiff, 1949.

Koehler, Ludwig, *Hebrew Man,* S.C.M. Press, London, 1956.

Kraus, Hans-Joachim, *Gottesdienst in Israel: Studien zur Geschichte des Laubhuettesfestes,* Munich, 1954.

———, *Die prophetische Verkuendigung des Rechts in Israel,* Theologische Studien, Heft 51, Zollikon, 1951.

Mendenhall, George, *Law and Covenant in Israel and the Ancient Near East,* The Biblical Colloquium, Pittsburgh, 1955.

Mowinckel, Sigmund, *He That Cometh,* translated from the Norwegian by G. W. Anderson, New York, 1954.

———, *Religion und Kultus,* Göttingen, 1953.

Niebuhr, Reinhold, *The Nature and Destiny of Man,* Vol. I, *Human Nature,* New York, 1941; Vol. II, *Human Destiny,* New York, 1943.

———, *Faith and History,* New York, 1949.

Noth, Martin, *Gesammelte Studien zum Alten Testament,* Theologische Buecherei I, Neudrucke und Berichte aus dem 20 Jahrhundert. Band 6, Munich, 1957.

Pedersen, Johannes, *Israel: Its Life and Culture,* Vols. I-II, London, 1926; Vols. III-IV, London, 1940.

Rad, Gerhard Von, *Studies in Deuteronomy,* Studies in Biblical Theology No. 9, translated from the German by David Stalker, London, 1953.

Ramsey, Paul, *Basic Christian Ethics,* New York, 1950.

H. Wheeler Robinson, *Inspiration and Revelation in the Old Testament,* Oxford, 1946.

———, "Hebrew Psychology," *The People and the Book,* edited by Arthur S. Peake, Oxford, 1925, pp. 353-382.

———, "The Hebrew Conception of Corporate Personality," *Werden und Wesen des Alten Testaments,* edited by Paul Volz and Friedrich Stummer, Berlin, 1936, pp. 49-62.

Rowley, H. H., *The Faith of Israel: Aspects of Old Testament Thought,* London, 1956.

———, *The Biblical Doctrine of Election,* London, 1950.

Ryder, Smith, C., *The Biblical Doctrine of Man,* London, 1951.

Tresmontant, Claude, *Essai sur pensée hébraïque,* Lectio Divina 12, Paris, 1953.

de Vaux, R., O.P., *Les Institutions de l'ancien Testament,* Vol. I., Paris, 1958.

G. Ernest Wright, *God Who Acts,* Studies in Biblical Theology No. 8, London, 1952.

————, and others, *The Biblical Doctrine of Man in Society,* Ecumenical Biblical Studies No. 2, London, 1954.

Index

155